The Nurse Who Sailed the World

Michael Page

The Nurse Who Sailed the World

Copyright © 2017 Michael Page. All rights reserved.

This work is subject to copyright. All rights are reserved by the Publisher, whether the whole or part of the material is concerned, specifically the rights of translation, reprinting, reuse of illustrations, recitation, broadcasting, reproduction on microfilms or in any other physical way, and transmission or information storage and retrieval, electronic adaptation, computer software, or by similar or dissimilar methodology now known or hereafter developed. Exempted from this legal reservation are brief excerpts in connection with reviews or scholarly analysis or material supplied specifically for the purpose of being entered and executed on a computer system, for exclusive use by the purchaser of the work. Duplication of this publication or parts thereof is permitted only under the provisions of the Copyright Law of the Publisher's location, in its current version, and permission for use must always be obtained from the Publisher. Permissions for use may be obtained through Rights Link at the Copyright Clearance Centre. Violations are liable to prosecution under the respective Copyright Law.

The use in this publication of trade names, trademarks, service marks, and similar terms, even if they are not identified as such, is not to be taken as an expression of opinion as to whether or not they are subject to proprietary rights.

Publisher: Elluminet Press
Indexer: James Marsh
Compositor: Luminescent Media
Type Setting & Layout: Luminescent Media
Cover Designer: Kevin Wilson

Introduction

Too unbelievable to be the work of fiction, these excerpts from diaries that I've maintained over the last few years tell of my travels working as a nurse across the world, on land and at sea.

Many people ask me why I ever became a nurse. I'm not sure, but it certainly wasn't for the reason once advocated in a British hospital by an elderly traveler lady in my care.

"You dirty bastard! You just like looking at old women's fannies! I'll kick you in the balls!"

WHACK!

As I'd been bending down to put her stockings on at the time I didn't manage to jump out of the way quickly enough.

After working as a qualified nurse for four years in British hospitals I decided that I needed to escape the infuriating web of rules and regulations within which these institutions have increasingly become enmeshed. Neanderthals placed flowers around their dead over thirty thousand years ago.

Hospital rule makers today tell us that we're not allowed to do likewise. I can only conclude that those hospital rule makers are more primitive and uncultured than Neanderthals. When I die I hope that someone has the guts to flout the rules and lay some flowers around me. By that stage I'm going to be a health hazard anyway, so a few flowers won't make any difference.

So why have I chosen to travail right across the globe? When I first qualified as a nurse I looked after an elderly lady patient who'd never been married or had children, but she'd had an interesting job and travelled widely. As she sat with her mobile phone and address book receiving a steady stream of visitors she told me: "Michael, I wouldn't have changed my life for the world." I often recount that story to my own daughter, adding: "You have one life, live it to the full." The British have always been a nation of travellers. Even now that our Empire which once covered a quarter of the globe has been whittled down to a few islands in the Atlantic the urge to travel remains cascading through the blood vessels of many of us.

So after qualifying I didn't take the conventional path like everybody else in my university cohort, becoming a staff nurse and then a charge nurse. I scoured the world looking for any and every exciting opportunity that I could grab with my qualification, never looking left or right at what others were doing or what they had, but instead looking at the horizon straight ahead of me, towards every opportunity available.

I hope that I've managed to capture snapshots of ways of life around the world that are fast eroding away, as developing countries like China quickly industrialise and the last places on earth cut off from civilisation are finally penetrated by roads, fibre optic cables and mobile phone masts. I also hope that I've managed to warn people about some of the many scams operating around the world so that they can avoid becoming victims themselves.

To those nurses who ask me what extra qualifications are needed to work in all the remote and dangerous places that I have, I reply: "gross stupidity." I'm one of those many nurses who has developed a "devil may care" attitude. We see so many people lost to cancer, heart disease and other conditions that we realise our time is limited and something will claim us sooner or later. The Grim Reaper comes for us all eventually. We spectate solemnly as hospital porters push away mortuary trolleys knowing that one day it'll be our turn to take a ride. So why not pack as much in as we can to whatever time we have, even if a degree of risk is involved? I've always wanted to travel to unusual places and have thus signed up to work in locations that have been well off the tourist trail, some of which have been amongst the most dangerous on earth. I've had a gun pointed at me, had pirates approach me, been lain up in bed with an unpleasant tropical disease and missed a multiple pile up on a dangerous road by inches. Only Lady Luck has delivered me safely this far. The British prime minister Sir Arthur Wellesley was born in 1769 and died in 1852. The British prime minister Neville Chamberlain was born in 1869 and died in 1940. I was born in 1969 and don't expect to live to see 2052 or even 2040. I'll probably die whilst working in some far flung corner of the globe, and indeed expect to be in such a place when this book is published. When it is, I'm sure that the same will be asked of me as of Darwin when "On the Origin of Species" was first sold. "Here's the book but where's the ape who wrote it?"

It's only as I read back through my manuscript prior to publication that I realise just how little work I actually did, and a friend who has proof read for me has concluded that I've done only one full day's work in the last few years. Much of the account that follows seems to be about my days off and getting up to no good. I don't know how I've managed to stay licensed as a registered nurse since 2003. Maybe once someone from Britain's Nursing and Midwifery Council reads this I'll be struck off the professional register?

So why did I write the book? Firstly, travel books on Saudi Arabia, Benin and North East Peru are relatively hard to find. So writing one will hopefully prove beneficial. Secondly I want to make readers laugh. As a nurse I believe that laughter is the best medicine. A hospital colleague once remarked that I made patients laugh so much there was a noticeable increase in wet beds and wet incontinence pads whenever I was on duty. I once had a whole bay of hospital patients laughing, then went off duty returning eleven hours later to find that one of them had died. Me making him laugh was the last thing that he experienced in this life, and this meant more to me than any successful resuscitation attempt to which I've ever been party. Thirdly I want to enlighten young people at secondary school as to potential career choices before them, some of which might take them around the world. I hope that, amongst the humour, I've managed to include some useful and serious information for young people considering a career; and that this book gives a more realistic, if grittier, insight into far flung corners of the world than the sterilised output of their school textbooks. I hope that this book doesn't put too many young people off a nursing career.

Qualifying as a nurse, teacher, engineer or in a similarly high demand discipline can enable those from poorer backgrounds to travel intrepidly and work across the world. More selfishly from my own perspective, many countries are already desperately short of nurses, the thousand or so hospitals in the British Isles alone being short of an average of nearly a hundred each. I certainly don't want to be waiting for hours for a nurse to be available to wipe my incontinent backside when I'm on my death bed.

I'm also working on an edition of this book that's suitable for children, and am in the process of removing all the references to prostitutes and drug misuse and all of the bad language. There was an enormous quantity of such material, primarily because of the gritty nature of both offshore and emergency medical work, and the tough, hard working, hard drinking, foul mouthed folks who in my experience seem to fill most of these occupations' vacancies. I'm probably locking the stable door long after the horse has bolted though. Most children have heard the "F" word hundreds of times by age eleven. I first picked it up when I was seven and my father was trying to tile the bathroom. I can't remember who received the biggest scolding from my mother, me for repeating the word the following day or my father when he returned from work to face accusations of teaching his son bad language. He denied all knowledge of wrongdoing of course. Thanks Dad, you dropped me right in it.

Spelling and grammar are always a sticking point whenever writing in English. One of my former offshore colleagues will no doubt chastise me for leaving the first letter of many nouns uncapitalised and starting sentences with "and" and "but." But unlike French, whose use has been governed by the Academie francaise since the seventeenth century, customs when writing in English are more fluid. Although I've been able to turn to an institution of reference in Paris to ensure that I've written this book's thirty or so French words correctly, no counterpart exists in London or Oxford for which I could have done likewise for the thirty thousand or so words written in English. Whenever we write in English we so often have to resort to asking ourselves: "Does this look right?" Many of written English's customs are at best open to interpretation and at worst illogical. For instance, why do some people but not others deploy inverted commas for the names of businesses or rock and pop bands? Why do most people capitalise the first letter of some rooms and job titles but not others? Why do most people capitalise the first letter of "euro," but not "pound" or "dollar;" and the first letter of "Jupiter" or "Venus" but not "sun" or "world," which are all planets? Moreover, English isn't one homogeneous language but a group that are very closely related and, most of the time, mutually comprehensible to its respective speakers. I'm preparing an edition of this book in American English, probably the most widely spoken of all of the language's derivatives. This edition, meanwhile, is very British. The book contains many references to British television, film and music which, rather than add footnotes, I'll leave the reader unfamiliar with our culture to google.

Although I've tried to exclude from this book anything that I feel is too personal, one individual who I can't fail to exclude from its contents is my daughter, who has provided me with far too much witty material for me to overlook her.

In several places in this book I make fun of people's attempts to speak English, but I don't feel that I'm being racist. After all, the Beninese and French laughed at my pathetic attempts to speak French in Benin. Sometimes we have to laugh at each other as well as ourselves, and I don't believe that doing so in such a way constitutes discrimination. Similarly my criticism of Saudi Arabia is not intended to constitute islamophobia, merely an attack on the Saudi authorities' vulgar interpretation of Islam that's so brutally oppressive towards anyone who isn't a heterosexual Sunni Muslim male, and even towards many of these too. As this book went to press it was finally announced that from 2018 women will be allowed to drive in Saudi Arabia, but the Kingdom still has far to travel along the road towards becoming a civilised country.

It's now time to recline your seat, relax and enjoy the journey.

Benin

Day 1

I'm destined for an oil rig off the coast of Benin, West Africa. Between the sixteenth and nineteenth centuries this coastline witnessed the abduction of millions of slaves, transported in abject misery, filth and cramped confinement on transatlantic slave ships. It's therefore highly appropriate that I'm embarking on the first leg of my journey aboard the twenty first century equivalent of a transatlantic slave ship, a Ryanair plane. Having been forced to pay a pound for a small plastic bag into which to place my toiletries, once airborne I use the last two pieces of paper in the plane's only working toilet. Due to Ryanair's minuscule luggage allowance I fly wearing three jumpers and three pairs of trousers, pants and socks. I arrive in Paris, ninety minutes behind schedule, dripping with sweat and resembling that well known French icon the Michelin Man.

The Air France flight from Paris to Cotonou, Benin's largest city, is less uncomfortable but eye wateringly expensive. Looking at Air France's ticket prices I can understand why the French have the same word for flight as they do for robbery.

I've visited Arab North Africa with its mosques, horse and donkey drawn vehicles and architecture influenced by both Southern Europe and the Middle East. But this is Black Africa, Africa south of the Sahara; predominantly Christian, infinitely poorer and with relatively few solidly built structures. Considering the region's poverty, animal drawn transport is notable for its absence. Here the motorcycle reigns supreme, and it's one such vehicle that takes me by surprise as I step out of the airport, almost running me over and putting me in hospital before I have any opportunity whatsoever to pick up a pen and start work.

I sleep little during the night before taking the helicopter to the rig. The penny pinching offshore contractor who has sent me here has billeted me in a hotel that possesses broken furniture and no functioning electricity. The company would have made me sleep on straw in a barn had they thought they could get away with it.

Day 2

The rig itself is no more comfortable than last night's hotel. I'm told that some rigs off the Norwegian coast now have saunas and jacuzzis. This thirty two year old tub doesn't even have a properly functioning plumbing system. I'm to share a three metre by three metre (nine foot by nine foot) cabin with three Frenchmen.

Some medical staff working in West Africa have questionable hygiene standards, and I open the sick bay's ointments cupboard to find that a used tube of Anusol piles cream has been returned with pooh around its end.

A colleague asks me why I have a box of children's dummies on the sick bay's desk. I've brought them because offshore oil workers are notorious for spitting their dummies out when they don't get their own way, and they're quite welcome to help themselves to a replacement. The dummies belonged to my daughter; but she, unlike the oilmen, has now outgrown them. How she graduated from the dummy stage of infanthood with any dummies left I don't know. One was thrown to a zoo's meerkats, another stolen by a monkey in Blackpool and a third stolen by a chicken, which promptly shot across a field with its prize in its beak.

Day 3

I'm up to start work at 5am after only a few hours' sleep. My three French room mates have been noisy well into the early hours. The French invented the guillotine. Had they invented a miniature one for a tongue, and had I held such a device in my possession, I'd have deployed it during the night. To add insult to injury one of my room mates tells me to speak to him in English because he thinks that my French is appalling.

I'm informed that today's dinner is turkey. I don't know what kind of exotic, endangered species of Sub Saharan African bird the caterers have decided to serve up, but it neither looks nor tastes like turkey, and has unpleasant adverse results on everyone's digestive systems. Intermittently, whenever I can liberate myself from the toilet, I spend the rest of the day issuing the crew with anti diarrhoearal tablets. I dispense these one at a time and ensure that each crew member swallows his tablet in front of me. I have no intention of half of the sick bay's pharmaceutical supply returning to land to be sold on a Cotonou market stall.

Day 4

I begin the day with a cup of coffee on deck at 5am. I'm so dependent upon coffee and cola to keep me fuelled up through a working day that I wouldn't last five minutes as a Mormon. And you could tar a road with the black coffee that I elect to drink, such is its consistency. My oesophagus and stomach are probably even more heavily tarred than a smoker's lungs. In my years at sea I've grown accustomed to drinking my coffee without milk. Fresh milk is very difficult to obtain outside of North West Europe and North America, although I did once hear of a ship working in the Middle East that carried a live goat on board.

I'm looking out for the rig's Client Representative, a seventy something eccentric relic of British colonial rule in West Africa. He should be easy enough to find. He'll be on deck facing the moon and barking at it.

Daylight breaks and a fellow Brit joins me on deck. I recount my room mate's unwelcome comment about my inability to speak French.

"He's right. I heard you over the public address system. You speak French about as well as the British policeman in the nineteen eighties television comedy 'Allo Allo.'" From that morning my nickname on the rig becomes Officer Crabtree.

The conversation then moves on to our health. Before I came out here I had to attend a travel health clinic for a John Prescott ("Two Jags"). One inoculation was against yellow fever and the other against diphtheria. It transpires that my colleague has travelled out here with no inoculations at all.

I hope that in the next few weeks he won't be in my sick bay dying of some fatal tropical disease.

My colleague casually propels his unextinguished cigarette over the side of the rig into the sea and a huge pool of oil drifting beneath us. I cover my ears instinctively, expecting us all to be blown sky high. My daughter, who at her tender age is already a most vociferous eco warrior, would almost certainly have had no reservations about complaining at the top of her voice. Being much more of a coward I say nothing.

To the left of the pool of oil I observe a stream of raw, untreated sewage being pumped straight out into the sea. I make a mental note not to swim at any of Cotonou's beaches when the helicopter returns me to land. The stream of brown liquid drifting out into the Atlantic Ocean confirms to me that yesterday's unidentified bird served up for dinner has had much the same effect on everyone's digestive system.

Two Beninese fishermen are casting their net from their little wooden pirogue a short distance from the end of the stream of diarrhoea. The second mental note I make is to keep fish off the menu while I'm in Benin.

I find a stretcher with no straps. Is the stretcher just hanging up for decoration, or is a casualty expected to cling on for dear life as he's manhandled around the rig and onto a helicopter?

Later that morning two Beninese workers are fired for trying to steal safety beacons. How reassuring it is that even the rig's safety equipment is being removed to be spirited away for sale. There's probably a street market in Cotonou with more equipment on offer from this rig than remains on board, and E Bay's "Rig Parts For Sale" section is probably also very well endowed right now. I glance over the side of the rig to make sure that its legs are still on.

I'm summoned to the rig's radio room to take a phone call from onshore. It's Timothy, who's the Onshore Controller at the helicopter check in desk.

He sounds indignant. "Michael, where were my sandwiches this morning?"

A subsequent investigation reveals that the rig's caterers have been sending sandwiches ashore via the daily helicopter to Timothy and charging the oil company over five hundred American dollars a month for the privilege. Meanwhile Timothy has been selling the sandwiches in Cotonou. This is West Africa. Everyone's on the make.

I'm gaining the impression that half the people with whom I'm having to deal out here are involved in a scam of some sort, using the Internet or otherwise. People back in Britain can't understand why I still do all my banking at the bank's counter, only send my curriculum vitae in response to specific job vacancies and never use social media. I feel not in the least deprived because I avoid social media's political and religious rants and public slanging matches. Others would understand why I take the precautions that I do were they to meet some of the tricky devils with whom I'm dealing now. Today's young generation, who across the world are welded to their little electronic toys as if they were some kind of life support machine, and who can't even start their dinners without taking photos of them to post online, are sitting ducks for any of this bunch of crooks who are running a scam involving the Internet. If you create a social media profile, the first people to look at it almost certainly won't be your friends or family, but some of the thieving cut throats who are now in my midst. Before you know it they've gathered enough information on you to hack and empty your bank account.

And it seems that every single man from Europe or North America who's working on this rig is running away from something, or someone, in his own country. If a taxman, divorce lawyer, private detective, judge or police officer is looking for a fugitive then I would suggest commencing the search on West Africa's oil rigs.

That afternoon it's announced that the tow boats haven't turned up for a scheduled rig move, ten kilometres (six miles) along the Beninese coast. I half expect to see workers produce oars to row the rig to its new location themselves. To start rowing would be just the kind of instruction that our "couldn't care less about safety" Rig Manager would give. He's so cavalier that I've nicknamed him King Charles the First.

A colleague who has English as a second language calls by my sick bay and asks me to proof read a report that he has had to write in English. It's only since I've started to correct my daughter's speech that I've realised how difficult a language English is to learn, and in particular how many irregular verbs it contains. The most difficult of all to master is that incredibly clumsy verb "to get," which is difficult to translate into other languages. Why couldn't Italian have been selected as the world's international language? It's a far more regular, rule adherent language and it has been the international language of music for centuries.

I've worked as more than just a document proof reader during my years at sea, and I've always enjoyed being called upon to be a nurse when someone becomes sick or injured but fulfilling many other occupations concurrently. The best thing about working as a seafaring nurse is that you're working where there are always plenty of other tasks to fulfil and where an extra pair of hands is always welcome. Over the years I've been trained how to erect scaffolding, operate ship to platform drawbridges and cook breakfast for fifty men. I'm not quite at the stage where I can climb into a drilling cabin, plunge a drill pipe into the sea bed and strike oil, but I think that it's only a matter of time before someone asks me to try. Even if there were ever to be no jobs for nurses I've acquired so many other skills that I'll never be out of work.

I also acquire a particularly useful function on board. One of the biggest problems is that the drilling crew, who are mainly American, can only understand imperial measurements. Meanwhile those crew who have English as a second language can understand only the metric system. I'm one of only two Brits on board, and seem to be the only person who can work using both systems. The crew therefore become increasingly reliant on their British nurse when they're drilling their holes in the sea bed. As far as learning both systems of measurement is concerned I was in the right place at the right time. Teaching metric measurements to British school children became mandatory in 1974, the year during which I started school. I still remember my infants' school teacher giving some pupils brand new red thirty centimetre rulers and others green twenty five centimetre ones. I also remember being bitterly jealous of the pigtailed little girl sitting next to me who was issued with a red ruler that was longer than my green one.

Day 17

At 1am I'm kicked out of bed to attend a casualty who has had a head injury and for two minutes lost consciousness. He must therefore attend hospital. I thus find myself outside haggling into my two way radio in my pathetic French trying to order a helicopter. The Beninese Operations Manager, worrying about the cost of a helicopter, tries to dissuade me from summoning one. By now I'm so angry, tired and frustrated that I switch into English.

"Get me that helicopter, because if I have to do it myself it'll be carrying two casualties instead of one!"

Although he can't understand English he can understand that I'm angry.

I appeal to the Rig Manager as he arrives on the scene.

"I need a helicopter to take my casualty to Cotonou University Hospital. I stand by my decision, even if it costs me my job."

I have no intention of finding myself in a Beninese court. In common with other former French colonies, Beninese law is based on French law, meaning that the accused is presumed guilty until proven innocent. Moreover, at this time, for those deemed to have taken a human life intentionally, Benin still has the death penalty.

My decision doesn't cost me my job, and at about 7am I receive an e mail from a hospital doctor who has received my casualty. She informs me that he's stable but that I made the right decision sending him in.

Emerging on deck, I spot a welder contentedly welding

away on an overhead walkway, sparks dropping around a drum of what looks like flammable liquid below him. Who's going to kill us all first, the welder, the caterers or the crew stealing the safety equipment? I would have hoped that after our head injury casualty safety would have improved, but it's the way of the world that some people never learn their lesson even after a catastrophe. I first went offshore as a nurse in 2007 to a North Sea oil platform close to the site of the Piper Alpha that had exploded nineteen years previously. I opened a stock cupboard next to the sick bay to find medical oxygen cylinders that hadn't been serviced for twelve years, and could have potentially fuelled a fire blowing the platform sky high. That platform's workers had clearly learned nothing from the Piper Alpha Disaster.

It's five days before I'm due to go home and I still have nobody appointed to relieve me. Vexed, I stare up to the top deck and the huge tank containing foam for use in the event of fire. The tank is labelled "SKUM" in one metre (three foot) high letters."Skum" is a brand name used for offshore fire fighting equipment. Right now though I feel like the rig's management is sending me a message. In the late eighteenth and early nineteenth centuries the British prison system housed convicts on vessels moored offshore that were no longer fit to sail. This morning I can relate to that.

I gaze out in despair over the Atlantic towards the Beninese shoreline. It was said in ancient times that sirens, beautiful nymphs, would lure sailors to their deaths at sea. Right now I'd jump overboard at the sight of any woman, even if she was pig ugly and weighed a quarter of a tonne, as long as she had a boat to take me to shore.

In desperation to find someone to relieve me in five days' time I contact my friend Graeme back in Britain. We worked together for years, including on a hospital ward where he hated Sister Mc Kenzie, the Charge Nurse, so much that he walked on duty one day demanding:

"Has anyone seen that ferret faced wee bastard?"

"Just who were you referring to?" Sister Mc Kenzie retorted.

"I was referring to you, you ferret faced wee bastard!"

At the disciplinary hearing that inevitably followed the staff were summoned into the room one by one.

"Did you hear Graeme call Sister Mc Kenzie, and I quote, a 'ferret faced wee bastard?'"

"No!"

"No!"

"I didn't hear anything!"

"Case dismissed. Graeme, you're free to go!"

Sister Mc Kenzie pursued Graeme out of the disciplinary hearing.

"I'll get you for this, you little shit!"

"Excuse me, would you mind turning round? The disciplinary panel are coming out right behind you and I don't think that one or two of them quite caught all of that!"

As a man who has extricated himself from many a fix I consider Graeme my ideal replacement in West Africa, even if he arrives and hates it so much that our long and valued friendship is sacrificed upon the altar of offshore expediency.

A crew member walks into my sick bay for the third time in as many days, announcing: "I have cough, I have body pains. I want antibiotics." In a British hospital I'd need a doctor's prescription before giving out any medication. Here anything goes, the expectation seeming to be that the crew member's medication of choice should be handed over with no questions asked. The demand for antibiotics doesn't surprise me. A packet can fetch a lot of money on a Cotonou market stall.

I look up and glance at him indifferently:

"Over the last three days you've had such an interesting array of minor ailments that I'm going to put you on a helicopter and send you to an onshore doctor. He'll then decide if you're fit enough to continue working."

The crew member scurries out of my sick bay without a word and never returns. Faced with loss of wages once leaving the rig, and a hefty doctor's bill, it appears that he makes a speedy and miraculous recovery.

Another crewman tells me that he has toothache. I tell him to come and see me about tooth hurty. Even if he understands the joke he doesn't laugh.

Later I'm sitting in the conference room. As I glance around prior to our operations meeting it appears that only about half of the crew have turned up. Conspicuous by their absence are the Dutch, Danes and Norwegians.

In all of their languages they say "half to the hour" instead of "half past." It later transpires that the meeting's time was mistranslated. They therefore turned up an hour ago, assumed that the meeting had been cancelled and went away again.

The Japanese Rig Manager appears having just conducted a rig floor inspection. His normally oriental yellow face is beet red with anger. To those of us assembled he proceeds to complain about one worker's toilet habits.

"What filthy bastard piss on wig fwoor?"

Nobody owns up.

Tonight I vow to remain in my bunk even if I am awoken at midnight, 2am and 4am by grown men who can't look after themselves. If they want their nose wiped or gender realignment they can wait until tomorrow morning. Some more liberal clinicians would term managing minor ailments with comfort measures and sympathy as "the placebo effect." In the middle of the night I describe them as completely unnecessary measures for a load of whining little babies who should have stayed at home with their mummies.

Day 22

It's 5am and the Rig Manager asks if I can stay on for an extra week because my relief hasn't turned up for the helicopter in Cotonou. He can whistle, which is something that we're not supposed to do offshore because it's supposed to bring bad luck, as if being here wasn't bad enough luck already. The superstitious believe that whistling offshore can whistle up a storm, and one gust of wind would probably have this heap of scrap metal capsizing into the Atlantic.

It's 11am and the helicopter from the rig lands back in Cotonou with me on board. In this devoutly Roman Catholic West African state the Beninese onlookers must think that I'm the Pope as I step off the helicopter and kiss the runway, so grateful am I to be back onshore. I take a furtive glance around to make sure that Northern Ireland's Reverend Doctor Ian Paisley isn't here to start screaming that I'm the Antichrist.

The two Beninese soldiers who have presumably been appointed to guard the airport have fallen asleep with their guns on their laps. If anyone wants to launch an airborne invasion of Benin then now would be an opportune time. Although I can't imagine that Benin possesses much to render an invasion worthwhile, which is presumably why these soldiers have assumed it safe to fall asleep.

My flight doesn't leave Cotonou Airport until tonight so I decide to head into the city. I walk the full distance into the centre and no bus passes me. A short way from the airport a rusting, French colonial metre gauge railway line curves in from the north to parallel the road.

Observing that the line's only visible rolling stock consists of a few decaying freight cars, parked in a siding, surrounded by weeds and each now appearing to be inhabited by several families, I quickly come to the conclusion that Cotonou has no local trains either. The Chinese are planning a new railway system for the region. I wish them luck. Most of the construction materials will probably be spirited away long before the first sod of earth is ever turned. This is West Africa. Anything of the slightest value not nailed down is gone.

Motorcycle taxis persistently swerve in front of me, at least two of them having hurtled down the wrong side of the road. They brake, sound their horns and tout for my business. Because these taxis don't even afford the pillion passenger the luxury of a crash helmet I keep walking. However depressed the last few weeks have left me I'm not quite ready to commit suicide in Cotonou's traffic yet.

The walk from the airport to the city centre is about seven kilometres (four miles), takes ninety minutes and isn't worth the trouble. Magnificent French colonial architecture Cotonou possesses not; only a scattering of ugly, concrete high rises, thrown up as if in a deliberate attempt to scar Benin's otherwise idyllic coastline.

As ibis rises in flight from a stinking, muck-clogged, litter-filled drainage ditch. How any wildlife has managed to survive in this closest vision I've ever had to the aftermath of the apocalypse beats me. On the opposite side of the road a man finishes urinating against a sign reading: "defense de uriner,"- "no urinating."

A decrepit Renault truck, probably dating from the nineteen eighties, negotiates the corner ahead of my path, narrowly avoiding shedding its load of plastic pipes that overhang the vehicle on all four sides and barely leave the driver room to observe the road ahead through the cracked windscreen. It's easy to see why West Africa has such a high road death rate. Some fatalities are even abandoned at the roadside for the vultures.

If a visitor is going to venture out and about in a dodgy, crime ridden country, the secrets are to do so only in daylight, keep moving, don't look at anyone, take photos as discretely as possible and don't drink any alcohol, especially if it's hot. Having walked so far though, I need to find some shade, crack open a cola and rehydrate. Unfortunately my need to stop has not escaped the attention of a local prostitute. As is common in West Africa, to get my attention she starts hissing at me as if she were a snake. Quite frankly I'd rather go to bed with a snake than with her. A nurse who spends much of his life at sea, with no other medically qualified personnel around him, soon learns to do everything he can to avoid going down with any disease, including a dose of the clap. I drink up quickly and walk on. My motto is: "non quaero tribulationis," -"don't go looking for trouble."

I had hoped to mail some post cards, but Cotonou's main post office is closed and looks like it has been for a very long time. I'm forming the impression that Benin has ceased to function since the French left. I have no more luck trying to find a functioning bank to exchange currency. As I brandish a wad of bank notes at retail outlets of various descriptions, indifferent shakes of the head meet my pathetic pleas of: "est-ce que ce n'est pas possible ici," –"isn't it possible here?"

As I've been writing this book I've even struggled to remember that the name of Benin's currency is the Central African franc. I used it so little because the country's shops contain so little worth buying.

I notice that the Beninese start saying "bonsoir"- " good evening"- a lot earlier in the day than I've been accustomed to in France. If this is because the Beninese like to go to bed much earlier than the French then that's understandable. Cotonou is no match for Paris' Montmartre or Moulin Rouge, or any town with one half decent pub for that matter.

Presumably in the hope that life will be better for West Africans in the next world than this, one thing that does function very efficiently in the region is religion. When one church preacher starts screaming into his microphone, another and another start to do likewise, until the whole town is alive with the preachers' defining cries. The situation is made worse because the local churches only have very thin walls and many aren't even fully enclosed.

I stop at small concrete hut to buy myself a cheese baguette which appears to have been baked in a charcoal fired oven. Walking round to the back of the hut I observe a herd of scrawny goats, grazing on a fly infested rubbish dump. Deducing the source of the cheese I'm sick in the weeds at my feet. It's a very unwell man who returns to Cotonou Airport that evening to board his overnight flight back to Europe.

Day 23

I arrive back in Britain just in time to pick my daughter up from pre school. Reunited after a long absence, I explain the plan for the rest of the day to her.

"You're having dinner with me and then you're going to Nana's and Grandad's."

"Don't want to go to Nana's and Grandad's. It stinks of cat pee. And I hope you're not going to give me a burnt dinner again, Daddy!"

"You'll eat what you're given. When I was in Benin I saw poor little children who would have been glad of your dinner."

"Well why didn't YOU give them something to eat, Daddy?"

I've nicknamed my daughter "Google." She has an answer for everything.

Saudi Arabia

Day 1

It's the day before I'm due to fly to Saudi Arabia to start work on a land based assignment as a nurse in a Riyadh hospital. I've spent the previous seven months running around London on an endless, fruitless merry go round of cosy chats and paperwork generation, to justify the ambiguous jobs of mindless bureaucrats with nothing better to do. The Saudi authorities have insisted on me visiting the London offices of a dozen different organisations before I've even been able to depart for the Kingdom.

My phone rings.

"Mr Page, I need to talk to you."

It's the so called "Coordinator." Having spent the last seven months trying to deal with this buffoon I now have little patience with him.

"I've got two minutes."

"You're not at work. Why have you only got two minutes?"

"Look mate, this is MY time. It makes no difference whether I'm having my portrait painted or sitting on the toilet, as long as I'm not doing both at once. I've got two minutes."

I learn from the Coordinator that tomorrow evening's flight has been moved forward to tomorrow morning. In the months to come I'm to learn that, to my misfortune, turning some poor unfortunate's life upside down with little or no notice is the way in which things are done in Saudi Arabia.

Day 2

Before I left Britain my daughter handed me a picture that she'd drawn. Entitled "FAMLIE," it depicted me standing in the top left hand corner, in splendid isolation, well away from anyone else. That's how I feel right now. Stepping into the forbidden Kingdom knowing nobody I must be the loneliest man in the world.

I've made landfall at Riyadh's Khalid Airport. When I was at university I had a landlord called Khalid. He owned our flat and the one downstairs. We paid fortunes in rent for flats so dangerous that an engineer once walked in, glared at the gas appliances and with the words "they'll kill you" shut off our gas. We resorted to cooking on a camping stove loaned to us by the local Scouts. Determined to get even, the night before they moved out the students downstairs shoved their flat's furniture into the back yard. Then they placed a life size inflatable doll from a sex shop dressed in their flat's curtains on top of the furniture, tipped petrol over everything and burned it.

Next morning, three hours after our neighbours' departure, my flat mate opened his window to find Khalid standing in the road with his arms up in the air.

"What's the state of downstairs like Khalid?" my flat mate asked curiously.

"They stole my curtains," came the pitiful reply.

Did the curtains contain thousands of pounds' worth of Khalid's ill gotten gains sewn within them? And does Khalid own this airport? The windows are curtainless. Maybe someone has made off with the curtains here too?

My mobile phone bleeps as I pass through the airport. The text message that I've received reads: "Welcome to Saudi Arabia." In the months ahead I'm to learn that the words "welcome" and "Saudi Arabia" never belong in the same sentence. The message would be more truthful were it to read: "You're only here because we're short of workers, infidel scum. Provided you don't say or do anything we don't like we'll put up with you and the Religious Police will leave you alone."

Whilst countries inhabited predominantly by Muslims such as The Gambia and Morocco abound with life, colour and vibrancy, Saudi Arabia must be the dullest, most restrictive, most depressing place on the planet. There's more freedom in communist North Korea. At least there alcohol, public entertainment and men mixing with women are all permitted. The world is more likely to see North Korea's President Kim Jong Un dancing Gagnam Style with Donald Trump than witness any dancing in Saudi Arabia at all.

Alcohol being illegal in Saudi Arabia, the very first thing I do is stop at a supermarket and purchase ingredients to make my own. Realising that most non Muslims do likewise, Riyadh's shopkeepers conveniently place the grape juice, sugar and yeast close together on their shelves. I've never tried making wine before but necessity is the best teacher.

I'm caught out by one of Saudi Arabia's infamous prayer calls, where the customer reaches the front of a line and the person who's supposed to be serving deserts his post and disappears for an hour. In theory this is to pray, in practice this is more often than not to skive off and have a sleep. Once the checkout opens again I pass through with vast quantities of grape juice, sugar and yeast. Nobody bats an eyelid.

Alongside the supermarket are several women's clothes shops, all displaying signs prohibiting the admission of males unless accompanying a female. In Saudi Arabia it must be almost impossible for men to either engage in transvestism or buy women clothes for their birthdays.

I buy a copy of Arab News, which I soon learn is the mouthpiece of Saudi Arabia's oppressive authoritarian government, much like Voelkischer Beobachter was in Nazi Germany. According to Arab News the United Nations has complained about the complete ban on religious freedom in Saudi Arabia, to which the country's authorities have replied: "All Saudis are Muslims." I can only assume that the Arabic words for "explanation" and "statement" are identical. I only retain this propaganda rag in case I find myself without toilet paper.

I pass a group of women who are out shopping in their abayas. These are long black capes that have to be worn outside by all women in Saudi Arabia. These lend groups of women the appearance of a swarm of giant mutant bats.

Day 7

I arrive at the Riyadh hospital to which I've been assigned. The place is vast. I make a note to bring pebbles to work tomorrow. Then I can do what Hansel and Gretel did in the German fairy tale and drop them along my outward path so that I can navigate back to my starting point.

"Is this room unisex? I don't want to be walking in on the female nurses in their frillies," I ask the female nurse directing me into the changing room.

"What makes you think any of us wear frillies?"

"You don't know what I'm wearing underneath" I reply. "You don't know the first thing about me. For all you know I could fancy the same blokes you do."

I've always been very fussy about changing rooms. Many hospital wards often have only one, the assumption being that all nurses are women. Years ago, on the very first day of my very first placement as a student nurse back in Britain, I waited patiently for the women to finish disrobing before entering the ward's sole changing room to change myself. When the women kept on walking in on me I complained to my nurse lecturer. She retorted, screeching at me in her pathetic, parrot like voice, face screwed up as if she'd just been in a high speed, head on car crash:

"I DON'T WANT TO HEAR AGAIN THAT YOU THINK THAT YOU'RE BEING DISCRIMINATED AGAINST BECAUSE YOU'RE MALE!"

It's an experience that I've never forgotten.

I have a training day. The Nurse Teaching Coordinator is conducting a lecture on epidural analgesia. I take knowledge of evolution for granted. I was educated at a London school where they knew they had to teach us about Darwin and evolution, because had they not we would have simply gone eight kilometres (five miles) down the road to Darwin's former country home at Down House and found out for ourselves. But I overlook that more than half of the world's children are still not taught about evolution and raise my hand.

"We can't insert an epidural infusion line between the lowest bones of the spine. Those bones have fused together as we've evolved from monkeys and lost the use of our tails."

The Nurse Teaching Coordinator glares at me with a face like an arse. I'm expecting to have the board eraser thrown at me.

"WE DID NOT EVOLVE FROM MONKEYS. GOD MADE US. CALLAS!"

I hear "Callas" a lot in Saudi Arabia. Dictionaries define it as "finished." But it's also used to mean: "this conversation is over," "I'm right, you're wrong," "don't even think about arguing with me," "shut up!" One two syllable word dashes all enlightened thought, dissent and any hope of Saudi Arabia ever progressing into the twenty first century.

That afternoon I'm invited to attend an "Islamic Cultural Awareness Workshop." Thanks for the offer, but I'll come on the day that members of the Saudi authorities start attending workshops on Christianity, Judaism, Buddhism, Sikhism, Hinduism and Shia Islam.

I send some e-mails back to folks in Britain, attaching a photo of a Thermoclock flashing at forty seven degrees Celsius. I caption the photo: "Don't you ever whine to me that you're hot again!"

Even though around half of Saudi Arabia's population is excluded from driving on the grounds of gender, Riyadh has been constructed with the motor vehicle in mind rather than the pedestrian. Entering and leaving the hospital as a pedestrian involves jay walking alongside and then across a treacherously busy six lane highway. I've been told about a nurse who left the hospital only to return by ambulance as a road casualty fifteen minutes later.

Walking back to my apartment, a colleague points out one of the apartment buildings reserved for male hospital staff, advising me not to visit unless I'm a homosexual wanting to be picked up. Although homosexual activity is still punishable by beheading in Saudi Arabia an underground gay scene apparently thrives, partly because contact between men and women is so restricted.

Not least because I've barely progressed from sending messages by carrier pigeon, I'm not a big fan of any phone. Rarely is the content of any received call more important than whatever you've had to break off doing in order to answer the phone. And I reserve a particular loathing for mobile devices, regarding them as necessary evils when engaging in foreign travel, but otherwise the instruments of control freaks to establish and maintain their empires and keep others subjugated. I've known one such control freak who has loved the sound of her own voice on a mobile phone so much that, on the rare occasions I've stirred myself into answering her calls at all, I've said "hi," set the phone on the table and returned fifteen minutes later to find her still gassing, oblivious to my absence.

The hospital now insists that I purchase a Saudi mobile phone, but in Saudi Arabia the control freaks are not only the phone owner's employer -and if they're particularly unfortunate any neurotic partner,- but also the government, who treat mobile phones as tracking devices for which the subject of surveillance pays for the privilege.

The kiosk's clerk begins entering my details on his computer. Purchasing a mobile phone in Saudi Arabia is no easy process. A buyer has to produce a forest's worth of paper documents before being fingerprinted.

"Your ID?"

I produce from my trousers something that no woman can possess: a Saudi driving licence.

" Your e mail address?"

"FU2 at writeme dot com."

My subliminal message to the Saudi authorities through my e mail address is lost on this man with very limited English as a second language.

As I leave the shop, new electronic gizmo in hand, I vow to disable the cursed device by dropping it in a bowl of water at the first available opportunity. If the hospital or anyone else is that desperate for me to be contactable at any time they can start paying me an "on call" allowance.

I attempt to drop off a small bag of laundry at a laundrette. The assistant, seeing what he falsely believes to be an ignorant but rich Brit who shits bank notes walk through the door, tries to charge me about three times as much as I would pay for the same bag of washing in Britain. I play the trick which I reserve for any situation where I believe I'm about to be ripped off. I produce only a small amount of money, deny that I have any more and leave the building. Never hand over a large denomination bank note in a country where you're liable to be cheated. You'll never receive any change.

During my tenure at the hospital I plan on seeing something of Saudi Arabia. So I visit a large bookshop that stocks publications in Arabic and English. As I peruse the bookshelves, notable for their absence are any political satire titles or anything likely to be critical of the government, any natural history titles that might imply the world is more than six thousand years old, any material that describes or depicts anything sexually explicit and any book concerning any religion other than Islam. All such books are banned by Saudi Arabia's censors. But I do manage to find a road map, which I promptly purchase.

Bahrain and Yemen were British colonies. So in the mid twentieth century they were equipped with British electrical systems and power points. The practice spread across their borders into Saudi Arabia. This now enables me to plug my British computer into a socket in my apartment and listen to Western music. I keep my apartment's windows firmly closed because the Religious Police will be round to smash up my computer if they hear what I'm listening to. As Saudi Arabia is ruled by a hard line Sunni Muslim dictatorship, perhaps "A Whiter Shade of Pale" by Boko Haram would constitute an appropriate choice of track?

Day 15

I have no experience of orthopaedics whatsoever, so the nursing agency that sent me here has in its infinite wisdom assigned me to an orthopaedics ward. Very few nursing agency staff are qualified nurses themselves. Half of all recruitment agents are sleazy, greasy sales reps who were selling double glazing before they started trying to sell people, only turning their hands to recruitment because they were no good at flogging double glazing. They have no understanding whatsoever of a job's complexities and are interested only in their next commissions. They have all the credibility, integrity and morality of Joe Walker, the spiv on the British nineteen seventies television comedy "Dad's Army." They puff themselves up by pretentiously calling themselves "consultants." But a consultant is a senior doctor, not a money grabbing telecanvasser.

As I arrive I notice that the staff nurses are undertaking all of what little work is being done. The Charge Nurse, who I'm to learn all too soon runs the ward like a commissar in charge of a Stalinist gulag, is busy at the nurses' station cutting out coloured craft paper and making decorations.

And guess who'll be doing the most work today? Finding that they now have a Brit in their midst, the Indians and Malaysians running the ward have decided that it's "pay back" time for the injustices of the British Empire.

They begin by plastering "reserved" labels all over computers, blood pressure machines and other equipment, so as to deny me use of them and prevent me from doing my job properly. What little electronic equipment is left available to me doesn't work. If I can't make a piece of equipment work I generally ride with the advice of the British band Status Quo, in their 1988 hit song "Burning Bridges." Turn it:

"On and off and on again."

But even this strategy fails. Saudi Arabia tries to project the image to the outside world that all of its hospitals possess state of the art electronic equipment. Electronic equipment they may possess, but much of it doesn't work.

None of the keys or combination numbers to the wards' medical supplies cupboards seem to work either. I vow that in future I'll come to work with a few sticks of dynamite so that I can just blow all the cupboard doors open. When I do eventually manage to open the cupboards I discover that there's no Pabrinex, thiamine or any other treatment for alcoholism, because in Saudi Arabia alcohol and therefore alcoholism officially don't exist. Perhaps the hospital authorities should try counting the numbers of people passing through supermarket checkouts with trolleys laden with grape juice, yeast and sugar? One cupboard does possess pregnancy testing kits but these are strictly for use on married women. Unmarried women are assumed to be sexually inactive.

I'm caught out by the ward's patient bed numbering system. In British hospitals patients' beds number from left to right. In Saudi hospitals, because Arabic script is written from right to left, beds number from right to left. As a result I almost start work on the wrong patient.

Anyone who has ever worked in or visited a British hospital will be well aware that those who have contributed to the British system through hard work will normally await their turn for treatment patiently. Meanwhile, unemployable layabout idiots who have chosen to land themselves in hospital through use of illegal drugs or other acts of gross stupidity will scream out demanding room service as if the institution were a five star hotel. The worst time of all to be working as a British hospital nurse is during Christmas Week, especially in Accident and Emergency. We see a steady procession of black eyes, stab wounds and casualties who have been glassed in the face with broken bottles, usually during drunken brawls between members of extended families. "Season of Good Will" my arse.

I'm to learn fast that in Saudi Arabia the situation is little different. On this ward the man constantly screaming out for room service is younger than me but looks eighty. He has apparently received no active treatment for months but receives regular doses of morphine at least five times higher than would be considered safe in a British hospital. In most countries such a patient would have long ago been discharged from a general hospital ward into a mental health facility, drugs rehabilitation centre or simply home and told to stop malingering. But this is Saudi Arabia. Anyone lucky enough to be the member of an elite family can demand more or less what they want. I wouldn't want to lie in a hospital bed for months on end, but, that said, this is Saudi Arabia. Perhaps there's less incentive for a patient to seek speedy discharge because there isn't a great deal that anyone's allowed to do outside anyway?

Is the country really so bad though that someone would want to spend months having morphine shot into his veins rather than face up to the reality of living there? Whether it is or not, discharge for this malingerer is liable to be on a mortuary trolley.

An intravenous drip isn't running through, so some basic schoolboy physics is called into play. Pressure exerted by a liquid equals H times rho times G, where H is the height through which the liquid falls, rho is the liquid's density and G is Newton's gravitational constant. In other words, if you want an intravenous drip to run through quickly, raise the stand to its maximum height.

The "crash" team are summoned as an elderly patient at the far end of the ward experiences a cardiac arrest. If I live past seventy and people start pumping me full of chemicals and jumping up and down on me for the sake of trying to offer me a few extra months of life, during which I'd only be lying inertly in a hospital bed, I'll be back to haunt them. When it's my time then it's my time. When it comes, for heaven's sake let me sleep.

I find myself assigned a Saudi male student nurse to babysit. This taking me by complete surprise I go to the office of the Nurse Teaching Coordinator, to ask what I should be teaching him. He sits me down and proceeds to lecture me for an hour on politics, religion and how much he hates the Jews of Palestine.

"Look, mate: I've got a student to look after and a mountain of work to do. The last thing I want to hear are the deranged ramblings of a reincarnation of Adolf Hitler!"

Eventually I manage to return to my student and we set to work changing a wound dressing on a patient. Nobody bothers to tell us that the patient's mate is about to enter the room, much less that the patient's mate is the King.

"Carry on working until we're told otherwise," I mumble to my student.

"But it's the King."

Unable to think of anything else to say, I recall a line quoted by Miranda Richardson, playing Queen Elizabeth I in Britain's nineteen eighties television comedy "Blackadder:"

"Either you can shut up or you can have your head cut off."

I try to carry on working whilst keeping a straight face. It doesn't help that last night I was reading about England's King Edward the Second screaming so loudly that he could be heard outside the walls of Berkeley Castle as he was tortured to death by having red hot pokers rammed up his backside. I'm now envisaging the same fate befalling the little man before me. My lack of concentration results in us making a complete pig's ear of the new wound dressing. I often think that I'm too cack handed to be a nurse. I once switched on the British nineteen seventies television comedy "Some Mothers do 'Ave 'Em" for my daughter, and she said of the accident prone dad who's the key character: "Frank Spencer's like you Daddy." Nevertheless the King must think we're doing a reasonable job looking after his mate. We reach the end of the shift with our heads still firmly attached to our bodies.

Up against some pretty stiff competition this is the worst hospital I've ever worked in for staff playing with their mobile phones when they're supposed to be working. Ostensibly the phones' calculators are being used for drugs calculations, but since when could Facebook tell you how much morphine to give a twenty kilo child? Many hospitals today have wards for alcoholics. I'm convinced that twenty years from now hospitals will have wards for people who've developed physical and mental health problems as a result of mobile phone addiction.

We return from lunch, in my case sandwiches, in my colleague's case Middle Eastern fava beans. As a result she proceeds to pass wind with enormous ferocity, standing next to patients as she does so, presumably in the hope that they'll take the blame. She'd get on like a house on fire with my daughter.

"Go and use the toilet please, those were absolutely horrible blow offs."

"Well they smell nice to me Daddy!"

It's just as well that this nurse wasn't at school with me. Where and when I was at school in London, passing wind could be punishable by Saturday morning detention, which encouraged us to keep our bowels closed at school from an early age. It could also lead to some highly embarrassing inquisitions. Early in 1986, when I was sixteen, we were all sitting in assembly, listening to the headmaster rattling on about nothing in particular. He had complete silence until a kid called Jerry Smy sitting at the back of the school hall let out a right, royal rip roaring blow off. It wasn't just a little one, it was "bang," and it echoed all around the hall.

I'm surprised he didn't pooh himself. He probably did. At the end of assembly two teachers came marching to the back of the hall and cordoned it off.

"RIGHT, WHO DID THAT FART?"

They never did find out who did it on that day and the older one of those two teachers died many years ago. But twenty four years later, and over six hundred kilometres (four hundred miles) from London, the younger one of those teachers was a headmaster at a school within walking distance of where I lived at this time. He persuaded me to come to his school for a careers day and talk to his pupils about my work as a travelling nurse. When I arrived I decided that it was high time I grassed up Jerry Smy. I never liked him anyway.

It's as I pick up the pile of assessment forms from the nurses' desk before me that I start to question the impression gained of British cities by doctors and nurses the world over. Bristol loans its name to a scale used by doctors and nurses to grade pooh, from lumpy to runny; and Glasgow loans its name to a scale of consciousness most commonly applied the world over to alcoholics and drug addicts. Another form concerns patients' pupils and I find it highly prejudiced. Apparently any patient whose pupils aren't of equal size isn't normal. I've always had one pupil naturally much bigger than the other. Am I normal? Maybe not.

"This is a weird hospital" my colleague sitting next to me remarks. "The doctor has written that the patient needs to see Psycho the Rapist and he has prescribed the patient sex in the day."

"Psychotherapist," I reply, "and 'sex in diem' is Latin for 'six times daily.'" The world over I don't know why they bother to send doctors to university. They never learn how to write properly.

I look round for the pen that I foolishly deposited at my side a minute earlier. It has gone. When will I learn never to put down a pen in a hospital?

I learn that I'm to receive an "outlying" patient from the gastrointestinal surgical ward. He has appendicitis, inflammation of that second stomach of which we've lost the use as we've evolved from grazing animals. But I dare not suggest this to the Nurse Teaching Coordinator and upset him again.

The patient is due for surgery. Although doctors and nurses in this hospital must speak English, many patients and visitors can't. I therefore look up "Nil by Mouth" in Arabic script using an Internet dictionary and carefully copy the Arabic script onto a bed end notice board. "I can't understand a word of that," remarks an Arabic speaking doctor. My idea to write in a foreign language has apparently been the worst since 1986, when a kid at school called John Fryer copied a story out of a German porno mag and handed it in to his teacher trying to pass it off as homework. He promptly found himself in Saturday morning detention alongside the farters.

I receive the patient's medication prescription chart ahead of the patient. Several items should have been given fifty minutes ago. This is not a problem. Nurses may give most drugs up to an hour either side of the prescribed time.

The logic here is that when we're working on ships we sail across time zone boundaries, and these distort timings for all purposes.

When my patient does arrive I have to take him to theatre immediately. I'm tasked with pushing him to an operating theatre on a trolley, or "stretcher" as they prefer to call it here. The generally accepted custom with trolleys in British hospitals' corridors is to keep left. Since Saudi Arabia is a right side driving country I can only assume that the custom here is to keep right.

I return to the ward to discover that women visitors have arrived clad entirely in black with only their eyes exposed. I advocate a more liberal dress code for women hospital visitors in Saudi Arabia, though perhaps not quite as liberal as exists in British hospitals. Why is it that so many women in their fifties visit their elderly parents in British hospitals dressed as right tarts, wearing short dresses and no tights? Is it a last act of daughter rebellion? You can see their knickers every time they bend over the beds. If the fifty something's daughter or granddaughter is visiting with her then the latter is usually more modestly dressed than her mother or grandmother. I've heard it said that those of us born in the third quarter of the twentieth century are the most rebellious generation in history. It's probably true. In Britain nowadays, grandparents are far more likely to listen to the punk band The Sex Pistols' 1976 hit record "Anarchy in the UK" on BBC Radio 2 than youngsters are on BBC Radio 1; and lyrics don't come much more rebellious than "I am an antichrist, I am an anarchist." Many of today's knicker flashing fifty somethings are the punks of the nineteen seventies.

I'm told to hurry up with my work, but I don't think that a hospital which keeps a patient in Accident and Emergency for twenty nine days is in much of a position to tell me to quicken my pace. Over the course of my life I've learned that those who are the most ready to criticise others are those who have the most faults of their own.

Although I'm not qualified as a paediatric nurse in Britain, here in Saudi Arabia I'm expected to look after the boys from new borns upwards. I utterly terrify the poor souls.

One little boy tugs at my stethoscope. I wiggle my right index finger at him.

"Out of bounds to busy little fingers!"

"WAAAAAAH," comes the response as the boy's expression mutates into one of terror.

Approaching a toddler with a nappy in one hand and a bag of baby wipes in the other, my exclamation of:

"HAVE YOU DONE POOOOOOOH?"

results in another wail of:

"WAAAAAAH!"

I then finish up with a crowd of Saudis around me. In this highly chauvinistic country they've clearly never seen a man change a baby's nappy before. The toddler emits a shrill cry of "Baba," which in Arabic means "Grandad." I still remember my daughter's first word being "dog," while we were passing a herd of cows. I'll accept both infants' approximations as good tries.

Another child, a neonate, hasn't yet been named. As I change his nappy I realise that he has been so full of shit he should be named after the Charge Nurse.

My uniform is soon covered in whatever the tots have chosen to expel from their little bodies. Tomorrow I'll come to work with a badge reading: "Hi, I'm Nurse Michael. Feel free to puke, pee and pooh on me."

A man wanders onto the ward and hands me a leaflet in English entitled "The Truth About Jesus." This describes Jesus' life according to Islam. In the open prison that is Saudi Arabia the Saudis don't miss a trick when it comes to high pressure sales techniques, trying to convert to Islam anyone whom they assume to be a Christian. It doesn't work the other way around though. A Christian giving a Muslim a Bible could face the death penalty.

I set up a patient's nebuliser. My first experience of such a treatment was when I was eighteen and became a patient myself. I was working on a children's residential summer camp near Birmingham. One of the other staff, an ex soldier whom it was rumoured had been dishonourably discharged, returned from the local pub at midnight very drunk. He put his military skills to use by making a home made bomb. It exploded in the staff quarters resulting in five of us going to hospital suffering from smoke inhalation. To this day I'm reminded of that night whenever I hear a nebuliser hiss.

The Charge Nurse must have flown home. There's no sign of her and from the window I can see no broomstick in the car park.

After my shift I go to the hospital canteen to meet some nurses with whom I've made friends. One of the girls complains that she's too fat to swim in her apartment building's outdoor swimming pool and that everyone would laugh at her. "I've never given a damn about what anyone thinks of me," I reassure her, "so you shouldn't care what anyone thinks of you. You'll be the one who's laughing after you've lost twenty pounds after three months of daily swimming. And besides, no men are going to see you in a pool because swimming here is segregated."

In the canteen the other nurses recount some of the hospital's more bizarre stories. One nurse asked a patient his occupation, to which he replied: "His Majesty's Executioner." Another looked after a Bedouin tribesman who, being unaccustomed to flush toilets, would wander out of the hospital to pooh in the sand, then wander back in again. A third was greeted by a family arriving by car with a dead relative in the back and expecting resuscitation to be performed. And together the staff tell me about a man sneaking into one of the hospital's "women only" apartment buildings concealed by a burka and abaya, so that he could spend the night with his girlfriend. The lovers were apprehended and thrown in prison pending deportation.

The assembled nurses also explain that, for the entire length of the Muslim month of Ramadan, anyone observed so much as eating a sweet or sipping water in public during daylight is liable to arrest by the Religious Police, the water ban in such a hot country inevitably resulting in a sharp increase in dehydration casualties admitted to hospital.

The Saudi authorities extend nothing like the same reverence to the Christian observance of Christmas, however. Anyone displaying a Christmas tree in their window is liable to a visit from the Religious Police to smash it up.

The hospital's detergents, combined with Saudi Arabia's extreme heat, are really drying my hands out. I'm using more Vaseline than a gay porno star.

Day 26

Because we run around crowded, noisy hospital wards for twelve to thirteen consecutive hours, unlike other workers most nurses like to retreat after work not to a gym or a noisy pub, but to the peace and tranquillity of their own homes, and I'm no exception. Moreover, very rarely do I watch television, and unless I'm at work or out in the evening I tend to go to bed quite early. I also usually rise quite early, finding the early morning to be the time of day when I'm at my most creative and therefore the best time to write, particularly at weekends when there's little traffic on the roads outside to interrupt my train of thought.

But 4.30am is a little too early even for me, and the ear grating warbling from the loudspeakers perched upon the minaret of the mosque across the road, which sounds like a cat being strangled, put paid to any attempt at activities entailing any degree of concentration. So I throw my pillow over my head and try fruitlessly to return to sleep. I vow that tonight I'll shin up the mosque's drainpipe and cut the wires to the imam's loudspeakers. In an era in which most devout Muslims have prayer call apps on their mobile phones it's hard to comprehend the purpose of these deafening screeches other than to satisfy the egotistical desires of any imam who loves the sound of his own voice. They say that it praises God. But is waking up hospital staff in the middle of their sleep cycle, before they go on duty to handle dangerous medicines that could kill patients if given incorrectly, a God loving act?

I always tell my daughter that parents, teachers and governments have authority over her only during her lifetime, that nobody has the right to tell her what religion, if any, she should practise, and that she should read plenty of books and make up her own mind about the potential destiny of her mortal soul. Such enlightened thinking wouldn't work here. In Saudi Arabia, every day of a person's life, hard line Sunni Muslim indoctrination begins every morning, sometimes as early as 3.30am.

The floor around my apartment's front door remains clear, as it does every morning, there being no door to door postal deliveries in Saudi Arabia. This means no junk mail, no letters threatening legal action if a bill hasn't been paid by this time yesterday and no political canvassing letters. The latter would be completely pointless anyway. Saudi Arabia possesses one of the world's most oppressive authoritarian regimes and there's no democracy here.

Leaving my apartment and walking across the pedestrian bridge traversing King Fahd Road I observe that "The Time has Come" has been sprayed on a wall in English. Somewhere in Riyadh there must be the beginnings of an anti government resistance movement.

I decide to take the second bus of the morning into Riyadh City Centre. I avoid the first bus as I'm reliably informed that it's always full of sick rubberneckers on their way to the ghoulish spectacle of the public executions.

As I wait for the bus at the roadside a taxi driver touting for business attempts to seek my custom by reversing into me. I've learned to avoid Riyadh taxis. Most have no working meters or seat belts and rarely does the driver even carry any form of map or other means of finding his way around. And if this taxi driver thinks that he's going to earn my custom by breaking my legs and driving me to the local hospital he's got another thing coming.

I work in the local hospital and having witnessed so many of its sharp practices I'd rather die in the street than die in there.

The buses are supposed to run every thirty minutes but I wait for over an hour. Presumably one of the Chinese pieces of tin foil that pass for buses in Riyadh has overheated and broken down in the scorching desert inferno that is Central Saudi Arabia.

Whilst Saudi Arabia's Islamic neighbour, Pakistan, has had a woman prime minister, here women aren't even allowed on local buses, although I think that few would want to ride on them. Men never form a gentlemanly line at bus stops, but push, shove and even hammer buses' doors open if they judge the driver to be tardy in opening them.

When I board every man on the bus stares at me as if he has never seen a European before. Years ago I met an elderly Russian man who started driving Moscow buses aged fifteen in 1934. The driver of this Riyadh bus doesn't look much older. Handing him two Saudi riyals I insist that he issues me with a ticket from the machine. Riyadh's bus drivers are notorious for pocketing fare money and handing passengers either used tickets or no tickets at all. My friend who works for the Saudi Arabia Public Transport Company has told me that, officially, only two thousand people a day use Riyadh's busiest bus route. But these figures are drawn from sales from buses' ticket machines. The true figure is probably closer to twenty thousand. This country seems to be riddled with corruption. I've seen beggars who have had a hand cut off, but clearly such a penalty imposed by the Saudi courts for stealing is insufficient to deter workers from putting their fingers in the till.

The bus pulls up at some traffic lights. Some poor unfortunate is fruitlessly trying to sell children's animal puppets to passing motorists. He has obviously just arrived in Saudi Arabia and hasn't realised that all public entertainments are banned, right down to children's puppet shows. Not a single motorist has the decency to wind down his car window and enlighten him.

It appears that the driver has decided to change the route of the bus. As he propels it at high velocity over a flyover I shout at him: "I want to get off at Chop Chop Square!" I mime being decapitated.

"Mafi Inglizi," -"I speak no English,"- he retorts nonchalantly.

By keeping the country's gates firmly barred to all but essential workers, Saudi Arabia's authoritarian government manage to project, through photos, television and film, the image of a country in which everyone lives in magnificent opulence, surrounded by sleek glass and steel skyscrapers, lush squares and fountains and highways clogged with top of the range four wheel drive vehicles. In reality the country is more on a par with India and Brazil. A few million people live in unimaginable luxury whilst many millions more, by far the majority, struggle to survive. Nowhere is this grinding poverty more evident than where I now alight from the bus, in Riyadh's central market area, Al Bat'aar. Here, predominantly foreign labourers live in dilapidated, jerry built apartment blocks, dissected by a labyrinth of rubbish strewn, unevenly paved alley ways which reek of stale urine. One location looks like it was struck by one of Iraqi dictator Saddam Hussein's scud missiles when he fired on Riyadh during the 1991 Gulf War.

Maybe the site will remain untouched for decades? I still remember a large World War Two bomb site in London that wasn't cleared and redeveloped until 1984.

I walk across Chop Chop Square, the public execution ground, to find two labourers hosing down the paving stones after the executioner's early morning blood letting. Nowadays the executioner lays down a large plastic sheet. After the execution, head, body and blood are enshrouded, thrown on the back of a pick-up truck, driven away and buried in an unmarked desert grave. Maybe this morning's executioner was a newly recruited amateur who missed the sheet and made a mess of the paving slabs?

Chop Chop Square contains the only popcorn stall that I ever find in Riyadh. In a country with no cinemas I guess that Saudis have to find a different spectacle to which popcorn can constitute an accompaniment? The sign hanging up in the square, in Arabic and English, reads: "My Prayers, My Happiness." What a lovely thing to read just before your head goes into the basket. Twenty first century Saudi Arabia sits uncomfortably and incongruously alongside the positively medieval. "'Ere's Mc Donalds, 'ere's Starbucks, 'ere's where they chop your 'ead off, mate!"

I stop at a café to buy a kebab. I don't know what exotic spices it contains, but it's hot, very hot. Observing that I'm eyeing the fire extinguisher, and presumably thinking that I'm about to rip it off the wall and drink its contents, a staff member brings me some water without my even asking. Later in the day, I'm convinced as a result of the kebab, I find myself crippled by diarrhoea. Considering the proximity of the restaurant to the public execution ground I shudder to think from where the café's owner obtained the dodgy meat.

Today I'm making a day trip to Damnam. My transaction at Riyadh station's ticket office is slow and cumbersome, but I'm used to that. Back in Britain I used to catch the train to work. The village station master, being a notorious hypochondriac and knowing that I was a nurse, would invariably complain of some minor ailment and expect me to examine him before he sold me a ticket.

My train is supposed to leave at 11.07 but at 11.07 is only just arriving into the platform. The train's tardiness doesn't seem to impinge upon the all male crew undergoing the ritual of jumping down from the train and greeting the all male station staff team with embraces and cheek to cheek kisses.

I board the "males only" carriage to find that there's a mosque on board. Muslims are supposed to pray facing Mecca. So what do devotees do when the train goes round a bend? Are they all supposed to shuffle round in synchronised formation?

It's 11.20 and the train still hasn't departed. My daughter once blew her toy whistle at a British main line railway station at the height of the evening rush hour, causing a stampede. Maybe I should have brought a whistle with me and tried the same technique here?

The train slinks out of Riyadh twenty minutes late. This isn't the latest running train on which I've ever ridden. That record is still held by one from Neuvo Loredo to Mexico City in 1991, which ran eight hours late because a bridge collapsed. Better late than never, I suppose. I'm sure that we'd have been more than eight hours late had the train been traversing the bridge during its collapse.

I sit back, relax and enjoy the journey as the traveller only can on a train. I prefer looking at what I've paid to see from the window to bursting for the toilet in a traffic jam or being relieved of a week's wages by retail outlets in an airport departure lounge. This is currently Saudi Arabia's only passenger railway line, although the government is planning more. There was a line from Medina to Haifa in what is now Israel, although this remained open for only twelve years before being destroyed during World War One.

Two North American diesel electric locomotives idle in a freight siding on the north side of the track. Portacabins, home to some of Saudi Arabia's millions of impoverished migrant workers, hug the south side.

Leaving Riyadh behind, much of the desert flanking both sides of the railway line appears to be under the stewardship of the petroleum giant Saudi Aramco. It's easy to understand why it's so much cheaper to produce a barrel of oil here than from beneath the depths of the North Sea. There's no need to drop a drill pipe down through hundreds of metres of water here, and no waiting days for wind and waves to subside before drilling can begin. According to Saudi Arabia's hard liners, God planted Saudi Arabia's oil beneath its desert for us in six days only six thousand years ago. So it shouldn't be too difficult to extract.

I pass through the women's and children's carriage. The stench of poohy babies' nappies being utterly overpowering I certainly think that the men have the better deal. A "Tom and Jerry" cartoon is playing on the carriage's television. The duo is immensely popular in Saudi Arabia.

Tom is always chasing Jerry around with an axe so he's probably now working for the Saudi government in a public execution ground somewhere.

A small, furry, white, ferret like mammal, which I have never managed to identify, scurries away from the train and into the desert. The sight of a ferret faced creature reminds me that I should really be phoning the Charge Nurse at my hospital ward.

I arrive in Dammam that afternoon. Someone reversing his car at high speed the wrong way down a divided highway misses me by inches as I walk away from the railway station.

Discovering that Dammam displays signs along the entire length of its sea front in Arabic and English reading: "No swimming, violators will be punished," I head along the coast to Half Moon Beach. Just as in Britain the summer crowds in seaside resorts such as Southend and Cleethorpes can be avoided by heading a short distance along the coast onto the marshes, so too can the hubbub of Dammam be escaped by travelling a few kilometres along the shoreline.

Leaving almost all of my ropy old body exposed, my Western swimming trunks are probably illegal, partly because this is Saudi Arabia and partly because of the revolting shape and complexion of said ropy old body. But there seems to be nobody around. So I take a risk, strip off and dive into the tranquil, azure waters of the Persian Gulf. No sooner have I done so then a swarm of jellyfish descend and sting me to within an inch of my life. Perhaps this is a form of biological warfare instituted by the Religious Police against anyone daring to swim in the near nude? I should swim more often.

Aged thirty one, I finally threw away a pair of swimming trunks that still had my name sewn within from my school days, so infrequent had been their use. But events such as today's offer me little encouragement to venture into water.

I return to my apartment in Riyadh late that night to find one of my bottles of fermenting home made wine has exploded with such ferocity that it has blown the cupboard door open and spurted across the floor then up the wall. The stench is overpowering, the temperature today having exceeded forty degrees Celsius. I dare not open the window though. Were the Religious Police to smell my half fermented moonshine I'd be dragged down to Chop Chop Square and publicly lashed.

Day 28

A combination of desert sand, wind and traffic pollution is making for a hazy grey day in Riyadh, so it's time to head out of the city. The car that I'm driving today is a Volkswagen Bora. I don't know how Volkswagen have managed to sell any Boras at all in the Middle East. "Bora" means "pooh" in Arabic.

Driving in Saudi Arabia is an activity from which a man can derive no pleasure whatsoever. Although women are banned from driving it seems that almost every male, from boys to old men, climbs behind a wheel, puts his hand on a horn, his foot on an accelerator and expects everyone else to get out of his way. And why vehicles in Saudi Arabia are sold with indicator lights I don't know. They're never used. An average of five people a day die on Britain's roads out of a population of sixty five million. An average of twenty three people a day die on Saudi Arabia's roads out of a population of only thirty two million.

This is going to turn out to be the roughest drive I've ever taken, with one exception. Back in Britain, spotting some fairground dodgem cars, my daughter recently insisted: "Daddy, I want to drive!" I still have the bruises from that escapade. When she turns seventeen her mother can take her on her first driving lesson.

My American friend and colleague has joined me for today's excursion. I've asked her to come with me because I feel sorry for her. On Saturdays in Saudi Arabia males are at least allowed to attend football matches and motor sports. Meanwhile females are kept under virtual house arrest. I'm wearing my hospital ID badge and she's sitting in the back of the car. This way, if the Religious Police stop me, I can say that I'm driving "this woman" on official hospital business. In Saudi Arabia females are not allowed to join unrelated males in cars for pleasure trips and under no circumstances can they sit next to an unrelated male in the front of a vehicle.

"Bear with me," I tell her. "I'm not used to driving on the wrong side of the car or the wrong side of the road."

"Why is it that you Brits think everyone else drives on the wrong side of the road?" comes the retort.

"Driving was on the left in Bahrain and Yemen before us Brits left."

"What has that got to do with anything?"

We drive out into the desert, the one place in Saudi Arabia where you can be whoever you want to be. There's nobody around to judge you for wearing whatever clothes you want, playing whatever music you want or consuming whatever you want. At weekends, which in the Middle East take place over Fridays and Saturdays, convoys of expatriates' cars head out into the desert to enable its occupants to misbehave away from the Religious Police's prying eyes.

Awareness of environmental issues in Saudi Arabia must rate as zero. It's quite clear that rubbish collected in Riyadh is simply fly tipped at the roadside in the desert. With little rain to break it up it may lie there for hundreds or even thousands of years. When the wind picks up a driver may need to use his windscreen wipers to combat a hailstorm of plastic bags blowing around in the desert.

We pass an articulated truck. The trailer is obviously a second hand British cast off. It can't possibly still be with its original owners because it displays an advert for British beer. A uromastyx, a yellow Arabian lizard resembling an iguana, scurries away from the car. A few minutes later my friend spots a herd of camels. Persuading me to pull over she promptly feeds our lunch to one of them. The camel sticks out its tongue and gives her a sloppy wet French kiss in return.

I've already mentioned that driving standards in Saudi Arabia are notoriously abysmal. To worsen matters, my friend sitting with her arm out of the window, her middle finger extended in that quintessentially American gesture of salutation that has in recent decades infiltrated Britain and other countries, isn't winning us any friends. So I jump at the chance when she asks if she can drive. It will give me a rest and keep her hands -and middle fingers- on the wheel. Taking what is probably the biggest and stupidest risk of my entire life I shift into the front passenger seat. It's probably more logical that the driving is undertaken by a woman from a country with two or three cars parked on every driveway than by a British man who rarely drives and doesn't even own a car. But I don't think that the Religious Police will take such a logical and enlightened view if they catch us.

Returning to civilisation we pull over at a souk, a Middle Eastern market. My friend insists that I try on an Arab head dress. Somehow I don't think that I'll make the next Colonel T E Lawrence, and I'm sure my friend still has the photos if she ever wishes to humiliate or blackmail me.

Before we leave she unhooks a light blue robe from the clothes rail. "No, you're not dressing me in that," I tell her. "It's too short for one thing. I'd look like the British nineteen eighties television comedian Kenny Everett's drag act, Cupid Stunt, and my appearance most certainly wouldn't be 'in the best possible taste.'"

A man stops my friend and complains that she's showing the flesh of her ankles and lower legs, in contravention of Saudi law. He doesn't understand much English. He certainly doesn't understand: "Get a life, you sad little man!"

Later on we try and find somewhere to buy something to eat. This is easier said than done because most cafés are for males only. My friend marches boldly into cafés only to be told: "No family, no family." Each time, I'm glared at, as if to say: "Why don't you keep this woman under control?" I glare back, as if to say: "You try!" My friend seems so determined to flout Saudi Arabia's draconian oppressive laws against women that I'm surprised she never gets us both lashed, jailed and deported.

Eventually we find somewhere that permits us to eat together, but we're penned into a little wooden booth like a pair of goats. The shame of a male and female eating together! Like many West Coast Americans my friend is a health freak and proceeds to lecture me on how my fried chicken, cola and chips —or "French fries"- are going to kill me very soon. "Do you want to be cremated or buried?" She asks. "Neither" I reply. "I've left my body to a university medical school for teaching medical and nursing students. While the rest of you are spending eternity in the freezing cold ground I'll be hanging up in a nice warm lecture theatre." Put off the contents of my plate completely

I throw them in the bin. I resolve to poison myself in peace in my own kitchen later on.

Out on the street I try to buy a packet of peanuts off a vendor, but it's during a prayer call and the religious police drive past us, heckling "salas, salas" - "pray, pray"- through their microphones. Both the street vendor and I could be dragged away for lashings in Chop Chop Square for trading during a prayer call, but the Religious Police are obviously in a good mood today and drive on.

Calling into a supermarket I face a stark choice. Do I spend a fortune on imported European groceries, such as the Dutch cucumber costing about seven times as much as it would in Europe, or do I make do with the local poison, such as Middle Eastern cheese, which tastes like shredded used car tyres? I steer clear of the chocolate aisle altogether. I've quickly learned that it's pointless buying chocolate in Saudi Arabia except for immediate consumption. It's the consistency of hot drinking chocolate within ten minutes of taking it outside, such is Saudi Arabia's heat. I carry my purchases to the automatic checkout machine. I usually avoid these cursed contraptions like the plague. Technology is sitting waiting patiently like a flock of vultures for my generation to die off before it takes over the world completely. I'm using the machine today for one reason only. Unlike a cashier, at least it won't tut and puff at me for paying for twenty riyals' worth of groceries with a five hundred riyal note.

My friend and I round a corner as we leave the supermarket.

"Michael, hold my groceries."

I then hear the sound of running water on the ground.

"You could have held that in till you got back to your apartment, you lazy, dirty cow! If the Religious Police come round that corner now they'll lash you on your bear backside. Your abaya's supposed to cover your entire body, but you don't even have your knickers up. Before I go anywhere with you in future I'm going to plumb you into a urinary catheter and leg bag."

Why is it that just because I'm a nurse some women consider it their prerogative to get on with the job right in front of me? And Saudi Arabia really needs to do something about its lack of public toilets.

Back at my apartment I decide that it's time to sample my moonshine, which has now been fermenting for four weeks. It's utterly foul, but the alcohol content seems to be sufficient. Many years ago I had a rabbit who waited until I put my glass of cider down on the living room coffee table, then stuck her nose in and helped herself. Nothing looks more funny than an inebriated bunny. Flossy lived to be nine so the cider can't have done her that much harm. I wonder what she'd make of my home made Saudi moonshine were she alive today? She was quite an affectionate little creature, although on one occasion she stuck her nose out towards me for what I assumed to be a kiss but instead she spat a rabbit dropping out into my mouth. What the gesture was supposed to signify I never did manage to ascertain. That bunny landed me in hot water many times. I once went to buy her a bale of hay, then walked straight into to the Saturday morning surgery of my local Member of Parliament unaware that he suffered from hay fever. On another occasion, whilst I was at work, I left Flossy in the care of a four year old girl. The two of them were playing together when a paediatric social worker swooped upon the girl. Far from being a nice lady, the social worker was of the same ilk as the net wielding Child Catcher from the children's film "Chitty Chitty Bang Bang." The rabbit bit her. Flossy was subsequently described in the family court as "a vicious creature that should be put down," a description that might well have been applied to the social worker. The bunny remained at large for the final eight years of her life, a fugitive from British justice.

Day 36

My favourite spot in Britain is Dalwhinnie. It's only just over two hours by train from Edinburgh or Glasgow, but where the forested mountain slopes cascade into the cold, crystal clear waters of Loch Ericht the traveller could just as easily be in a remote region of Canada or New Zealand. Central Saudi Arabia has nowhere remotely approximating to Dalwhinnie. It possesses no lakes or forests, even in the desert the traveller is rarely out of earshot of the mosques' incessant prayer calls, and there's no prospect whatsoever of a Highland malt scotch whiskey in a local pub.

Moreover, whereas in Britain people run out of ideas for things to do indoors because the country has too many cool, wet and windy days, in Saudi Arabia people run out of ideas for things to do indoors because the temperature climbs to over forty degrees day after day and most people find it too oppressively hot to venture out.

But all of the above notwithstanding, I'm so fed up with being stuck indoors that I decide to risk dying of dehydration or skin cancer by making a day excursion by coach to Al Kharj, eighty kilometres (fifty miles) south of Riyadh.

More fool anyone who turns up for their coach ten minutes before departure. Security at the coach station is as tight as at any airport, with bags having to be checked in and both bags and passengers scanned.

Although they're not permitted on local buses, women are allowed on coaches. They and their male chaperones board through the front door and other men board through the door in the coach's centre. Today a single man has inadvertently sat in the women's and chaperones' section at the coach's front. The driver unceremoniously shoos him, protesting, towards the rear.

Arriving in Al Kharj to find the town about as attractive and as interesting as a pan of boiled potatoes, I decide to take a walk in the surrounding desert. As I do so a Bedouin tribesman emerges from his tent and pursues me with his staff, heckling me. Maybe he thinks that I want to steal his goats?

Finally ridding myself of the irate tribesman I seat myself under an acacia tree whose leaves have become too depleted by the local camel population to offer much shade. I'm immediately attacked by a swarm of biting ants. It seems that every living thing in this desert wills my departure.

I always work on the assumption that smokers are never fit enough to walk more than a few hundred metres from a vehicle and that the presence of cigarette ends on the ground therefore indicates the close proximity of a road. I'm correct. As I complete the ascent of the rocky ridge before me Al Kharj lies sprawled below as untidily as if it were a four year old's first attempt at town planning. It probably was. I've walked in almost a complete circle.

Back in Al Kharj I stop to buy a hot dog. Pork being illegal in Saudi Arabia the sausage is beef and possesses the consistency of malleable plastic. Having bought a return ticket for the six thirty coach back to Riyadh I ensure that I'm back at the coach station half an hour before departure.

The ticket clerk shrugs his shoulders.

"This coach not run any more. Next one tomorrow morning."

"What? Then why the blazes did your colleagues at Riyadh Coach Station sell me a return ticket for the six thirty departure?"

Why can the British travel writers Michael Palin and Michael Portillo always reach their destinations successfully but not this Michael P? Perhaps if I first became a failed British politician I might then become a more successful traveller?

But I need not have despaired. The clerk refunds the cost of my ticket and, with true Middle Eastern ingenuity, walks towards the main road, flags down a passing motorist and persuades him to take me back to Riyadh for the coach ticket's price.

Day 54

Today I'm in Hofuf, or Hfuf, depending upon which signpost you read. Because the Arabic alphabet has no vowels the translator can be highly creative when transliterating Arabic words into Latin script. I'm in the caves that were reputedly inhabited by Ali Baba in the story "Ali Baba and the Forty Thieves." I don't know how many thieves that Saudi Arabia possesses today, but I've met more than forty already, at least half of whom have succeeded in ripping me off. Rather than explaining how geomorphology has sculpted the caves over millions of years, which would be forbidden in a country whose authorities refuse to accept that the world is more than six thousand years old, the tourist information boards instead display Koranic verses, turning the caves into something of an Islamic theme park.

On the street near the caves I watch as a plastic bag is furtively exchanged for bank notes. Another transaction involving illegal home made alcohol has clearly just taken place. Whilst I'm quite happy to let friends partake of my moonshine within the confines of my apartment, and I'm now even conducting lessons in my kitchen for my friends in the production of illegal alcohol, I won't let anyone take booze beyond my front door. The risk of being caught by the Religious Police is both unnecessary and too great.

Back in Riyadh I attempt to return north to my apartment in one of the city's battered, decrepit, death trap, privately owned Toyota Coaster minibuses. These are little bigger than a European Ford Transit seventeen seater minibus, but drivers will attempt to cram up to thirty men within. Anyone who can't obtain tickets to watch the racing cars in Bahrain should come to Riyadh, whose minibus drivers drive faster, not to mention more dangerously. The driver spots a bus that has been heading south but has now broken down, leaving a couple of dozen passengers milling around at the roadside. Realising that this is a business opportunity not to be missed, the driver performs a breathtakingly dangerous U turn across the six lane highway, turfs the five of us off who are on board and begins to admit the southbound passengers from the defunct bus. Such is Saudi Arabia's public transport system. I walk the rest of the way home.

I arrive back at my apartment to find that someone has shat outside of my front door. Either that or one of the local cats has learned how to use toilet paper.

I re enter my apartment having been away for a few days to discover that I forgot to empty the washing up bowl before I left. With the windows having remained closed, the air conditioning switched off and the indoor temperature having climbed above forty degrees in my absence, the dishwater has turned stagnant and my apartment now stinks to high heaven.

I can imagine that life in Saudi Arabia today is somewhat akin to what life was like in Nazi Germany. I can certainly understand why the Nurse Teaching Coordinator feels so at home here. In particular I've become convinced that the elderly, robed, bearded concierge at my apartment building is a stool pigeon and spy for the Religious Police, and that he's now keeping me under surveillance to try and catch me making alcohol and receiving unrelated women visitors. (My documents state that I'm a single male living alone, so I can only legally receive male guests in my apartment).

However, any rebel living under a totalitarian regime soon dreams up ingenious ways of circumventing the system, and I've learned to sneak my alcohol ingredients and friends in and out of my apartment during Saudi Arabia's incessant prayer calls. At these times I know that the concierge will be devoutly bowed on the ground in the direction of Mecca. I also take the extra precaution of putting my front door bell out of action. This is easy enough. The cowboys who wired it up have done such a shoddy job that all I have to do is tug at a wire hanging down the wall. For such craftsmanship I pay as much in rent as I would for an apartment in most British cities that would be three times as big and have infinitely higher safety standards.

It's my birthday. Highly appropriately, given my age and that everyone thinks I'm a grumpy old man like its key character, Victor Meldrew, I've received a boxed DVD set of the British nineteen nineties television comedy "One Foot in the Grave." How it was smuggled past customs, the censors and the Religious Police beats me. I don't believe it!

My "pay advice," sent to my phone, indicates that I've received a wage cut for the second time since arrival. As is customary in Saudi Arabia this has been completely unannounced, and in a country with no trade unions an employer can pursue such unscrupulous practices with complete impunity. I'm now earning little more than I would as a nurse back in Britain.

Day 92

My visa has forbidden me from leaving Saudi Arabia for the first three months of my stay, but now that three months have elapsed I make good my escape. I've heard it said that some British hospitals are a big pile of crap. If so then at least they're a big pile of British crap. And there's a lot to be said for wallowing in British crap rather than becoming mired in crap elsewhere, which can prove to be ten times smellier and a hundred times more difficult from which to extricate oneself. If there is any moral or message in this chapter it's that one should try travelling and working elsewhere in the world because it may spawn an appreciation that what one has at home isn't perhaps quite so bad after all.

I've ridden to Riyadh's Khalid Airport for my flight home. In the departure lounge a young woman of about eighteen has just ripped off her black abaya, which now lies abandoned in a heap on the floor looking like a dead cat. She now sits wearing a short skirt with her legs apart, knickers on view to the world. It's as if she's giving the Religious Police the finger, saying: "I'm leaving Saudi Arabia anyway. What are you going to do about it?"

It's time to start looking for a new job. As I wait in the airport I phone a worldwide recruitment agency called Michael Page. When I tell them that my name is Michael Page they think that I'm having a laugh. I also use my phone to look up an organisation on the Internet that I know is seeking nurses, but Saudi Arabia's censors have blocked the web page because it has "Christian" in the title.

The very last thing that I do before I board the plane is to send an anonymous e mail to the management at the hospital where I've been working, detailing all the corruption and sharp practices that I've observed during my time there. I use a fake e mail account and write in American English. Hopefully one of my American friends will be blamed.

Having not seen rain for months, once I'm back in Europe I plan to go outside during the first spell of rain and dance. Such an act would be forbidden in Saudi Arabia whatever the weather. I won't pretend that I've liked the country, and by writing this I'll probably precipitate Saudi Arabia's swiftest book banning and burning since Salman Rushdie's "The Satanic Verses" in 1989. But whenever my life runs badly, including whenever I leave a bad job in a bad country, I see it not as one door closing but many others begging to be opened. I'm the eternal optimist. I'm always prepared for the worst but hope for the best.

Crossing the border from Saudi Arabia into Qatar, and changing planes in Qatar Airport, I buy and sample my first legal alcoholic beverage for three months. It costs about three times what it would have done in Britain but it's worth every penny.

Day 96

A few days after I return to Britain I receive a letter asking if I'd be interested in another nursing contract in Saudi Arabia. I drop it straight into my box for outgoing mail with an FU2 postcode, in other words the bin.

Rather than sit at home watching the rain wash down the windows I go out and find something to do. Better a cold, wet and miserable country with plenty to occupy me than a hot, sunny country that possesses almost nothing. I visit my local supermarket where an alcoholic who recognises me as one of his nurses from a local hospital approaches me and shakes my hand warmly. I'm not setting him a very good example. Making up for lost time after teetotal Saudi Arabia I've piled my trolley high with beer.

An Ocean Voyage

Day 1

I arrive at my Scottish port of embarkation to learn that the ship to which I'm assigned hasn't yet docked, meaning that I'll need to amuse myself today. I don't need to visit the shops or bank. I ensured that I did so before I travelled, because today is a Monday. As a rule, if you're in Scotland on a Monday, assume that it's a local public holiday and local businesses will be closed. Whereas everywhere in England and Wales observes the same eight public holidays each year, in Scotland public holidays vary from place to place, although some businesses observe the same holidays as the rest of Britain. Yes, it's confusing, isn't it?

One task that I have overlooked before going to sea, however, has been to seek a haircut. I thus stop at a sea front barber's, probably the only place on the British coastline nowadays where there's no chance whatsoever of bumping into the long haired "Coast" television presenter Neil Oliver.

The sea looks enticing for bathing in the warm June sunshine, but I know that appearances can be deceptive. Particularly at higher altitudes, temperatures in Scotland on a summer's day can drop from above twenty degrees to below ten degrees in a matter of hours. Moreover, in the Northern Hemisphere's temperate regions, seas are at their warmest in early September and coldest in early March, meaning that sea temperatures in early June are about the same as in early December.

Within an hour of my arrival it has started raining. I dive into a café for cover. The radio is playing the British band Supertramp's 1982 hit record "It's Raining Again," which might as well be Scotland's national anthem. I order a glass of cola and am charged more than double the going rate in Britain. No wonder Scotland has such a problem with alcoholism. Such extortionate prices offer the drinker little incentive to switch to soft drinks.

English school children have always taken their summer holiday between July and September. This is because the majority of England's farms grow arable crops and, until mechanisation in the third quarter of the twentieth century, needed children to help with the harvest. Being cooler and damper, Scotland possesses mainly livestock farms that never required the same degree of seasonal labour. Scotland's school children thus commence their summer holiday in June. A girl of about fourteen, who has presumably just started her school holiday and is bored already, sidles up to me and starts trying to chat me up, asking if I have a girlfriend. Do all teenage girls in this town have a penchant for older men? Envisaging the gates of Peterhead Jail opening up before me I politely make my excuses and make a sharp exit.

Overlooking how hard it has been raining I slip and fall on my way out. I check myself for broken bones. If I could sue the café the sheriff court might just about award me enough compensation to buy one of the café's colas.

I try to navigate by the sun whenever I can, keeping it on my back if I want to walk east in the afternoon. But this form of navigation is entirely impractical in places where the sun rarely shines. Giving up trying to find the docks on foot I manage to find a bus to take me there. The driver seems in no hurry to arrive though, preferring instead to waste time engaging in a slanging match with a prospective passenger.

"Where's this bus going?" a woman demands as she tries to board.

"What has it got on the front, hen?"

"Yer miserable bastard!"

"If yer think that's what it has got on the front hen, yer'd better get yer eyes tested!"

"Yer stupid old bastard!"

"I'm nae stupid, hen. I run this thing for the likes of you who's too thick to pass a driving test!"

"Yer miserable bastard!"

"I'm nae miserable, hen. Look, I'm smiling! I'm enjoying this! Come on, let's 'ave some mer."

"Yer shite!"

"Is everyone else enjoying this?"

Several passengers at the back of the bus cheer. The woman isn't impressed.

"Yer's slags, the lot of yers!"

By this point the driver has had enough.

"I don't like yer language hen, that's why yer's walkin'. Tattie bye!"

Closing the doors and pulling away from the kerb he turns to address his passengers.

"Right, hands up who votes we go round the block and see her again?"

Such conflicts on land remind me why I occasionally feel the need to escape to sea.

A foreign tourist performs a graceless tumble whilst descending the stairs. This is a common occurrence in Britain. As small children, Brits master the art of balancing whilst using staircases on moving double decker buses. Citizens of most other countries, which don't possess such vehicles, often acquire a few bruises when attempting a British double decker bus journey.

Alighting at the dockyard I turn my attention to finding my ship.

I embark that evening. As is often the case the North Sea is rough. No sooner am I aboard than the crew queue up outside of my sick bay for cetirizine, an anti motion sickness tablet. I've been going to sea for some time but still suffer from occasional seasickness. I avoid the cetirizine though.

It causes drowsiness, I'm on twenty four hour call and I know that the next twenty four hours will be busy. I'm also handed the poison chalice of allocating cabins to crew members. Offshore this is often a task handed to the nurse, partly because it's assumed that the nurse has little to do and partly because nobody else wants to do it, since most crew members are never satisfied with their cabins.

Having had no time to undertake any laundry before leaving home, I throw every item of clothing I have, except what I'm wearing, straight into the ship's laundry room. My clothing is returned six hours later, unwashed and bound in grey tape. The laundryman has scrawled irately along the tape in black marker pen:

"You're taking the piss!"

Within an hour of casting off and heading out into the North Sea we have a lifeboat drill. It may be June but it's still cold. It never ceases to amaze me how many crew members emerge on deck for late night or early morning North Sea lifeboat drills wearing only shorts and T shirts, and that I don't have to treat a dozen cases of hypothermia after every such drill.

It's after ten in the evening, but this is Scotland in June and therefore we still have broad daylight. When I owned a house with a large garden in Scotland this was the time of year that I dreaded. I would return from weeks working abroad to find that the garden's grass, weeds and nettles, nourished by nineteen hours of daylight and Scotland's incessant rain, would have grown to the extent of turning my garden into a jungle.

Day 2

We head south through the North Sea. The tail of a whale, which I'm guessing is a minky, breaks the surface. I'm gutted that I'm so slow with my camera.

Up on the bridge the Captain is slumped in his seat with his feet up on his control panel, letting the ship's computers do all the work. Nowadays when on the high seas ships more or less steer themselves. I hope that the computer controlled navigational equipment is effective. We're fairly close to the shoreline and the British Isles has some of the largest tidal ranges in the world. Water depths in the same location can thus vary immensely from hour to hour.

I'm having a particularly bad day, a crew member having fallen from a considerable height in a store room. Casualty evacuated, I'm sitting in the sick bay in the middle of seeing another patient when the Assistant Operations Manager bursts in and starts ranting and raving, firstly at the patient who should have been at a meeting, and then at me for seeing the patient when he should have been at the meeting. Standing up, I walk towards the Assistant Operations Manager, who starts to back out of the doorway. I'm determined to give back as good as I've received.

"How was I supposed to know that he should have been at a meeting? And you DON'T burst in here while I'm seeing a patient."

By now, we're both standing outside the sick bay, surrounded by onlookers.

Ten minutes later, a plump little deck hand, who reminds me of Lofty on Britain's nineteen seventies television comedy "It Ain't 'Alf Hot Mum," waddles up to me and taps me on the shoulder.

"Everyone's so pleased that you stood up to that arrogant arsehead."

"Have you got any matches?" I reply. "I'm just about to perform Scotland's first witch burning since 1698."

I'm pleased to have made a friend among the crew even if I've made an enemy out of the Assistant Operations Manager.

As I make my way down the corridor the Norwegian chef stops and asks me if I think that the crew members attending the meeting will need feeding this evening.

"The Assistant Operations Manager does," I reply curtly, "preferably overboard to the sharks."

Later, the chef tells the Assistant Operations Manager exactly what I said. A Norwegian word that entered the English language in the mid twentieth century springs readily to mind: "quisling," another word for traitor.

Day 9

We're in Castillon de la Plana on the east coast of Spain. I ride inland on a trolleybus, a form of transport of which Britain's streets have been devoid since 1972. I know a secondary school boy who's being trained as a trolleybus conductor at a British museum by a man in his eighties. There's nobody with the necessary experience available to train him who's any younger. Apart from one of Western Europe's last trolleybus systems the town possesses little of note. So I don't linger for long.

Day 14

As we approach the Tunisian port of Zarzis a small boat packed to the gunwales with passengers passes us. These are probably migrants attempting to flee in search of a better life in Europe. Leaving Zarzis Docks I'm passed by a convoy of cars with Libyan registration plates, roof racks dangerously overloaded with personal effects. It seems that Tunisia is full of desperate people trying to get out and even more desperate people trying to get in.

Fellow passengers boarding a local bus direct me in through the rear doors, where a conductor sits patiently at a cash desk waiting to take my fare. Everyone around me is speaking Arabic, but, since Tunisia was a French colony, French is widely spoken in this North African country. It's in this language that I now request my ticket. Unfortunately the French word "sud" –"south"- is mistaken for the Arabic word "souk" –"market." So I head off in an unexpected direction to an unexpected destination.

The presence of so many soldiers and military vehicles indicates our proximity to Tunisia's border with strife torn Libya. So too does the souk bereft of tourists.

Back on board the ship I learn that two Brits have been fired for consuming alcohol. Valuing my job too much to risk dismissal I always restrict my shore leave treat to a large ice cream. They can't fire me for developing diabetes.

Day 20

Somewhere in the stretch of Mediterranean between Tunisia and Malta I spot a large sea turtle from the deck. I'm told that nowadays such a sighting in this region is rare.

I'm granted shore leave when we dock in Valletta Harbour, Malta. Walking down the gangplank towards the dock gates I observe a line of beautifully decorated forty year old, British built AEC Swift single decker buses decaying on the quayside. I recognise them as the buses that I used as a child in London in the nineteen seventies, after which they were exported to Malta and adorned superbly by local artisans. Malta has had fifteen hundred years of Arab heritage. The Arabs used to decorate their camels in beautiful, vibrant colours, and the tradition continued when camels were replaced by trucks and buses. Now the multinational transport operator Arriva has just taken over bus operations on Malta, introducing its drab, standard issue aqua and cream buses. Meanwhile Malta's superbly decorated customised buses are consigned to decay on the dockside. A multinational company has wiped out fifteen hundred years of Arab heritage in Malta in one night and is probably oblivious to having done so. Moreover, the buses recently introduced onto Malta's roads are cast offs that Londoners didn't like because their engines kept on overheating and blowing up. Shipping the buses to a much hotter country where the engines now blow up even more frequently seems to have been a highly logical solution.

I pass through the dockyard gates waving my passport and British Seaman's Discharge Book. It's Saturday afternoon, there's sport on the television and the security guard doesn't even look up from the screen. If any terrorist is planning on entering any country anywhere in the world and launching an attack he should enter through a small dockyard on a Saturday afternoon during a sports fixture. He could walk through the dockyard with a bomb under his arm warbling "death to all unbelievers" and the security guard still wouldn't notice.

At a currency exchange office I hand over a wad of twenty pound notes that I've brought from Scotland. I ask for euros. The clerk examines my Scottish bank notes suspiciously, then holds them to his backside and mimes wiping himself:

"You can go to the toilet with this money."

I can understand Scots' resentment whenever they travel anywhere, including England. Few people outside of Scotland will accept Scottish bank notes.

Day 26

The Eastern Mediterranean island and former British colony of Cyprus feels a little bit Greek, a little bit British and a little bit unique. The ship is thirteen days late, but since Cyprus' Eastern Orthodox Church runs thirteen days behind the rest of us, we are, according to the Julian Calendar, docking in Larnaca dead on time. Until the early twentieth century some governments in Eastern Europe were still using the Julian Calendar for all official purposes. I once encountered a very elderly patient in a British hospital who had two different dates of birth, thirteen days apart, logged in the hospital's records. One date was according to the Julian Calendar and the other the Gregorian. The patient had been born at a time and in a place in Eastern Europe when the Julian Calendar had still been in use.

At 7am the dockyard's foreman, an ex British Army officer, has us all lined up on parade. He marches up and down shouting and bawling as if we were a bunch of renegades newly recruited into the army. This daily ritual is rather too affectionately known as "Penguin Parade." But if the keepers at Scotland's Edinburgh Zoo were to shout and bawl at the penguins in the manner that the army officer now shouts and bawls at us then they'd be facing charges of animal cruelty.

A cock starts crowing in a back garden adjacent to the dockyard. This provokes a predictable stream of double entendre from the army officer about a cock coming out.

We start work. Amused, the Cypriots decide that my name sounds like "Muddy Face" over the two way radio. This immediately becomes my nickname.

At lunchtime the army officer marches into the dockyard office in which I'm working.

"Muddy Face, get your good for nothing arse out of here, you lazy bastard!"

For a moment I think I've been fired. But it transpires that he's halting operations and giving everyone the afternoon off.

The phone rings as I'm leaving. Stopping to answer it I take the caller's message, which I then relay to the army officer.

"It's Reggie. Wherever he is he says he's 'left knickers here.'"

"Nicosia, Muddy Face! It's the capital of Cyprus. Go on, clear off!"

I'm permitted the use of one of the company's four by four pick up trucks, so I head north. After about half an hour the road comes to an abrupt halt. Upon a barbed wire fence strung across my path signs in Greek and English read: "Area under Turkish Occupation."

Turning west I drive up into the mountains and end the afternoon in a hillside taverna. The sign outside reads "The Orange House." This conjures up images of an Ulster pub into which I once walked that had been turned into a shrine to King William of Orange, the Dutch homosexual whom Ulster's homophobic Orangemen revere incongruously. Men dressed in their daft little black and orange pixie costumes returning from a parade were throwing darts at a photo of the Pope on the dartboard. But this Cypriot Orange House couldn't be more different. It offers a comfortable seat with panoramic views across the island's central mountain range. However, a bottle of water costs more than a bottle of wine. If Jesus came here then economic common sense would dictate that he should change wine into water rather than vice versa. But I'm driving, so I resist the wine.

Day 35

As we sail further east I notice that the crew's behaviour is starting to deteriorate; the rigid, stoical formality of offshore life in the North Sea giving way to something more akin to a group of overgrown boys on a school trip.

The ship docks in the port of Abu Qir, near Alexandria in Egypt, location of Admiral Lord Nelson's Battle of the Nile. The island near the mouth of the harbour is known as Nelson's Island.

Being granted shore leave, and in the hope of finding something to do in the city, I sit at one of the ship's computers. I google "Alexandria," but this isn't much help as Alexandria is one of the World's most common place names. There's one in Scotland and even one near Washington DC.

I stroll out of Abu Qir Dockyard. I overlook the fact that in Egypt driving is on the right hand side of the road, even though the country was once a British protectorate. Consequently I'm almost mown over by the first vehicle that I encounter.

It's Sunday morning, the start of the working week in the Middle East. A horse and cart load of little children, immaculately turned out in navy blue school uniforms, passes by. It's the first of many horse drawn vehicles that pass me. They're still common in Egypt. Britain's roads looked much the same until not that long ago. I know people my own age who as children had their milk delivered by horse and cart as recently as the nineteen eighties. When the rain starts to lash down in sheets many of Egypt's roads flood and motor vehicles come to a standstill. As the roads start to flood I come to appreciate the advantage of this timeless form of transport as I watch the horses trot effortlessly through the flood waters.

I pass a pick up truck which is conveying the most bizarre combination of cargo I've ever seen: two goats and a wheelchair. Chuckling, I envisage an elderly Egyptian sitting in his goat powered wheelchair, holding a set of reins and ordering his steeds to "giddy up."

I enter Abu Qir Station. Spotting me photographing a train a railwayman gestures to me. It looks like I'm in trouble.

"Come!"

But then his earnest expression melts into a smile. He beckons towards the train's driver's cab.

"Today only, train for you FREE!"

I make that morning's journey in the driver's cab in the company of the driver and his assistant. I try to converse but that's easier said than done. Egypt's railways were built by the British, but the majority of its locomotives today are North American, old, poorly maintained and exceptionally noisy. Egypt's railway system is in a decrepit state. I travelled around Mexico by train before the government shut down the country's entire passenger railway system in 1997. I'm now wondering if the same fate is soon to befall its counterpart in Egypt.

The branch line running south east from Memora Junction traverses the marshy reed beds of the Nile Delta.

The window of the train reveals a spectacle that could have been drawn straight from the Old Testament of the Bible. Indeed, it's this very Sea of Reeds that scholars now believe Moses and his followers traversed to escape Pharaoh's army of charioteers.

The train leaving Edku is so full that passengers are riding on the locomotive. I somehow manage to squeeze into one of the passenger cars. But I'm riding next to sliding doors which don't close, so I'm clinging on for dear life trying not to fall out onto the track.

That afternoon I visit Alexandria. Alighting from the train at the city's main railway terminal I complete my journey to the city centre by tram. Unknown to me the conductor charges me for two people and presumably attempts to pocket the extra fare money. But a sympathetic passenger spots what he's doing, calls him back and makes him return his ill gotten gains to me.

One of Alexandria's barbers not only cuts the hair on my head but also "threads" the hairs in my ears and the excess ones around my eyebrows with a length of cotton. It's unfortunate that I've never encountered a barber since who has been able to replicate the practice, my unwanted hairs having grown back thicker than ever.

That night, returning across a pitch black dockyard, I fall down a metre (three foot) deep hole. Limping back to the ship with a sprained ankle I find myself confined to my sick bay as my own patient.

The ship's Polish Captain takes little interest in my predicament. He has had troubles enough of his own. "Mikey, harbour master keep telling me: 'Move ship, move ship.' What he think this is, a moped?"

Day 46

I conduct my weekly first aid practice on deck. Lying down, I beckon to a crew mate.

"John, I'm unconscious but breathing. Show me what you'd do."

John turns his back on me, puts his hands in his pockets and walks away. How very reassuring. Let's just hope that I don't lose consciousness on this voyage.

The laundryman comes to tell me that I now have the cleanest mobile phone on board and takes great delight in presenting it to me personally, along with the pair of trousers in whose pocket it entered the washing machine. Never mind, you can't often get a mobile phone signal at sea anyway.

The food has almost run out. Breakfast cereal and noodles are all that remain. Having lived off these and these alone for several days I don't want to see another noodle or piece of breakfast cereal as long as I live. One crewman quips that The Law of the Sea should now prevail and we should draw straws to ascertain who should be eaten first.

We must be approaching land. Nowadays the sighting of plastic and other human detritus on the water's surface indicates an approach to land long before the shoreline comes into sight.

Day 53

The ship casts off at dawn from Abu Dhabi and by day's end is sailing along the Iranian coast.

A Danish crew member turns to me:

"My mobile phone has just bleeped. I have a message that reads: 'Welcome to Iran, Danish traveller.'"

I stare incredulously.

"Presumably it then goes on to read: 'We haven't forgotten the Mohammed cartoons published in a Danish newspaper and the Ayatollah Khomeini Memorial Death Squads are now tracking your mobile phone signal?' I suggest you switch it off before they send a boat out here, catch you, put a rope around your neck and hang you from a construction crane in a Tehran square with everybody gaping at you."

We're flanked by Iran on one side of the Persian Gulf and Saudi Arabia on the other; two countries whose regimes detest each other, if only because they're in such intense competition for who can have the world's most appalling human rights record. Anyone who fancies taking the ship into a port on either side of the Gulf and going ashore for a beer can forget it.

I spend the afternoon checking the emergency medical kit carried in the FRC. In the offshore oil and gas industry the abbreviation "FRC" stands for "fast rescue craft." The same abbreviation is also used to denote any crew member who's getting on others' nerves, "R" in that instance standing for "rude." As a rule I hate abbreviations as they mean different things to different people.

For example, "EMU" means "early morning urine" to doctors and nurses, but something else to a banker, something else again to a railwayman, and to a zoo keeper it's a large, flightless Australian bird.

Day 56

My turn to stand on deck and look out for pirates comes around whilst we're somewhere north of the Maldives. Pirates are still found off much of Africa's coast and some of Asia's and South America's. As a child I grew up with the cartoon pirates Captain Pugwash and Master Mate. (The narrator's nasal voice made "Master Mate" sound like something else, which resulted in an unholy row culminating in the series' creator taking British newspapers to court). But the pirates whom I'm seeking today aren't "yo ho ho and a bottle of rum, shiver me timbers" jolly tars with parrots on their shoulders and eye patches. These mean cut throats carry AK47s.

About an hour into my watch I spot a small boat astern, on the horizon, approaching us at speed. I radio the Captain who in response accelerates the vessel. The small boat arcs around and heads away from us.

The verdict is that the little boat probably did convey pirates, but that our ship was moving too fast and is too heavily fortified with barbed wire around its decks for them to attack. When I first qualified as a nurse I never expected anything like this in my career because pirate attacks don't tend to take place on British hospitals. I can't wait to tell my daughter that I've seen real buccaneers. She can now attend fancy dress parties attired as a pirate "like one of those who tried to get my Daddy."

More commonly associated with centuries past, pirates remind us, as we switch on our televisions and the world's latest conflict is beamed into our living rooms, that strife worldwide is nothing new. Humankind has known pirates, thieves, conflicts and killing since time immemorial. Throughout human history someone has been aiming weapons at someone else somewhere. In the words of the American singer Billy Joel's 1989 hit record: "We didn't start the fire. It was always burning since the world's been turning."

Day 65

A barbecue is held on deck. As we eat, the Filipino catering crew serenade us with the aid of a karaoke machine, murdering hits by Elvis, the Beatles and others. Meanwhile frigate birds circle the ship, eyeing the karaoke singers as if to regard them as a giant evolutionary step backwards from themselves.

Day 78

We've weighed anchor in the Johor Strait about three kilometres (two miles) off the coast of Singapore. Some of us are heading ashore. Although the city state has the birch and even the death penalty for some offences it exhibits a remarkable tolerance of prostitutes, and a queue quickly forms outside of my sick bay for barrier contraception. I'm loathed to supply this, partly because I know that most of these men are married and partly because having to sign out so much medical stock and order more creates a lot of extra work for me. As I hand out the contraception I have to laugh when one seaman tells me that, on a previous visit to Singapore, he went to bed with a prostitute whom he believed was female but turned out to be a lady boy.

Whilst the others head for the infamous "Four Floors of Whores" in Singapore's Orchard Road, I'm going to content myself with a visit to the zoo, and contemplate all the cases of the clap that I'll be treating later in the voyage. I agree to meet the others in a bar later. The difference between the zoo and the whorehouse is that the zoo animals are far more selective about where and when they mate, and with whom. A toothless tinker, doing the rounds of the ships in the Johor Strait in his decrepit little wooden motor boat collecting scrap metal, bares a mischievous smile at us, points in the general direction of Orchard Road and makes a sexually explicit gesture with his fingers. Everybody laughs.

Once ashore I look around for something to eat. A few of the older streets in Singapore, with their colonial architecture and double decker buses, have a positively British feel about them. In one such street I stop at a stall to buy something that I've never tried before- fried insects. I take one bite and expel my entire mouthful straight out into the gutter.

Day 79

It's midnight in a Singapore bar. Fresh from the whorehouse Martin, probably the wildest member of the crew, tries to persuade me to become a "true seaman" and receive a tattoo. Anyone who thinks that I'm turning myself into a walking billboard has another thing coming. Some dads can only remember their kids' birthdays by having them emblazoned on their skin, but I have no trouble remembering my daughter's birthday, thank you very much.

A crewman is so drunk that he falls asleep at his table in a corner of the bar. Four other crew members line up next to him, face the wall, pull down their trousers and pants and bear their backsides. Meanwhile someone else takes a photo. An incensed bar maid comes over wiggling her finger:

"You is velly bad mans!"

Meanwhile an even bigger exhibition is being made by the ship's Danish Chief Officer. This is the same man who plays Dido's song "I will go down with this ship" rather unsettlingly on the ship's bridge at the start of his every watch. Tonight he's standing on a table, brandishing a wine bottle and singing: "I am a Viking!" He's certainly making a complete Cnut of himself.

Cnut, incidentally, was the Viking king of Scandinavia and England a thousand years ago, when he was the world's most powerful man, much as Donald Trump is today. A thousand years separate these two most powerful men of their eras, yet they're known by almost the same name.

It's 1am, and on the way back to the dockside the Chief Officer throws his wine bottle in the bushes, spits on the ground and urinates against a wall. Each of these offences carries a thousand dollar fine in Singapore. So I hope that he has deep pockets if he has been either spotted by a police officer or caught on a security camera.

Half an hour later a motor launch takes us from the dockside back to our ship, moored in the shark infested waters of the Johor Strait. It takes three of us to manhandle the intoxicated Chief Officer off the motor launch, up the gangplank and over the side of the ship. It's the most dangerous thing that I've ever done.

The Viking King Cnut is perhaps best remembered for sitting on a beach and believing himself so powerful that he could prevent the tide from coming in. I smile as I think of Cnut while three of us stand on the ship's bridge and scour tide tables, as well as fuel logs and Admiralty charts. If the Chief Officer hasn't sobered up by dawn we might have to sail this thing ourselves. I've never had to learn how to read Admiralty charts, the general assumption being that the sick bay will, hopefully, sail in the same direction as the rest of the ship. But right now I think that even I could make a better job of skippering this vessel than the inebriate in our midst.

Here in the waters of the Far East nobody seems to care how much alcohol a man has consumed. Alcohol is strictly prohibited in the oilfields of Britain's North Sea, which results in North Sea oilmen arriving back in Aberdeen after weeks without booze. Consequently they drink southbound trains' buffet cars dry by Stonehaven as they head home. Maybe trains' buffet cars wouldn't be drunk dry so quickly if alcohol were to be allowed in the North Sea?

By 11am the photo of the drunken crewman and his four backside bearing colleagues is the screen saver on every computer on the ship.

Two men alight from a motor launch, board the vessel on the port side and make their way towards the bridge.

"Who are those guys?" I ask a fellow crewman.

"Bastards," he replies.

These are Singaporean customs officers coming aboard to conduct an inspection. Having read the sign "Warning, death for drug traffickers under Singapore law" on the dockside, I scurry down to the sick bay to scour the controlled drugs register with a fine tooth comb and ensure that what's in the register tallies with what's in the stock cupboard. I have no wish to end this voyage swinging from the end of a rope in Changi Jail. The Ancient Mariner had a dead albatross hung around his neck. Today the albatross around my neck is the key to the sick bay, which right now I wish was anyone's responsibility but mine.

The ship's Chinese Client Representative stops me:

"What time ship sail?"

I smile wryly:

"You have many proverbs in your country. In mine we have one too: 'In the wild and wacky world of offshore the only certainty is that there are no certainties.'"

The Client Representative hastily tries to punch my proverb into his mobile phone.

Day 103

The food on board in recent weeks has been foul. This lunchtime's fare has consisted of what has resembled -and probably tasted- like starling marinated in wallpaper paste. Taking matters into his own hands a crewman casts his fishing rod over the ship's stern into the South China Sea. He catches a huge tuna, turfs the catering crew out of the galley and cooks and serves up the best meal we've had since Singapore.

Day 106

We land at the Southern Chinese port of Zhanjiang. Since I'm about to be granted a full day's shore leave I switch on my e mail's auto response: "If you're the Chinese government snooping at my e mails I hope that you're enjoying what you're reading. Free Tibet!"

As I stand on deck whilst the ship docks I'm confronted by the awe inspiring sight of what appears to be a production line of offshore oil platforms, each in various stages of completion. The platform at the "finished" end of the line is perched on top of a giant barge, awaiting transportation out to sea. Such has been the breakneck speed of China's industrialisation in recent years that the country now possesses an insatiable appetite for fossil fuels.

There is now so much interaction between Britain and Poland that my daughter is friends with as many Polish children as British ones, and there are as many flights from some British airports to Polish cities as there are domestic flights. But it wasn't always that way. In 1990, when I was twenty, few Poles knew any Brits and vice versa.

It was in this year, just after the Berlin Wall had fallen and the former communist countries of Eastern Europe had ceased to be all but off limits to Westerners, that I travelled across East Germany and Poland to Warsaw. I exchanged each pound in my money belt for sixteen thousand Polish zloty, Poland having experienced rampant inflation in the period before my arrival. And for two days I stayed in the apartment of a Pole my own age. I remember vividly the forest of identical, drab concrete apartment blocks, mile upon mile of them, within which he lived.

Zhangiang's dockside suburb of Potou evokes memories of that time in Poland through its regimented rows of drab, concrete apartment blocks, with their utilitarian communist architecture, that flank the road from the dockside. The blocks each consist of eight storeys, eight being a lucky number in China. To be allocated an apartment on the eighth floor is considered by the superstitious to be very lucky indeed, but since few of these buildings contain lifts I'd beg to differ.

On the dockside I have my first customer, a young Chinese university student working as a watchman while our ship is in port who has sprained his ankle. I apply some ibuprofen gel, enshroud the ankle in a Tubigrip compression bandage and advise him to visit his local hospital if there's no improvement in seven days. The young man retorts that his parents could not afford to pay a hospital bill for him. To this I express surprise that, in a communist country, he would have to pay. It seems that we Brits have the best of both worlds, democracy but also free medical care that one might more closely associate with a communist regime. As I tend the young man we have a long conversation about economics, science and sociology that I'll never forget.

If there's one thing that my work abroad, and in China in particular, has taught me, it's that, far from their populations living in mud huts with low levels of education, rapidly developing countries around the world are turning out many millions of highly skilled university graduates each year, intensifying competition across the globe for the best available opportunities. I don't envy my daughter's generation of young Brits. The fight around the world among school leavers and university graduates for the best jobs in the early twenty first century is becoming far more intense than it ever was in the late twentieth, when in the decades after our Empire's demise many Brits clung doggedly for too long to the perception that British was best.

The port agent pulls up to collect, amongst other things, a bag of expired medications for disposal from my sick bay. The ship subsequently receives a bill of fifteen hundred American dollars for him having performed this task. And I'm betting my life that the port agent takes all such medications not for incineration but to be flogged on a local market stall.

My day's shore leave beginning, I stroll out of the docks, hail a bus, drop three Chinese yuan in the driver's fare box and ride across the new suspension bridge spanning the river into Zhanjiang City Centre.

In 1982 China's President Deng Xiaoping announced that "to get rich is glorious." Since then rich Chinese seem to have applied some interesting but lurid spins on to how to flaunt their wealth. One particularly plush but gaudy looking new apartment building has a base designed to look like a pagoda but its upper storeys resemble those of a New York skyscraper.

Sitting opposite me is a young woman with her new born baby. Cecil Rhodes once said: "To have been born British is to have won first prize in the lottery of life." That may have been the case in the nineteenth century. Today though, as I recall Rhodes' words whilst gazing at this adorable new born, and then at the labyrinth of new buildings, many still in various stages of construction, flanking the highway along which we now pass, I cannot help but think differently. In the twenty first century the first prize in the lottery of life will surely, in due course, be handed to China's present generation of infants.

It's the weekend and the main shopping area of Zhanjiang is thronging with parents out with their child. To stem China's phenomenal population growth, in 1980, Dung Xiaoping introduced a "one child per family" policy; although in recent years, here in Guangdong Province, the policy had been relaxed to permit the birth of two children per mother, providing that neither parent has a sibling of their own.

Zhanjiang is a quirky place. On one side of the main road stands a new indoor shopping centre, containing a Walmart supermarket with goods labelled in Simplified Chinese and English. On the other, by the river, stands the fish market. Were it not for their outboard motors the gaily painted little wooden junks unloading their catches at the quayside could pass for being hundreds of years old. The city was a French concession during the European colonial era, but throughout my time here I see neither a baguette nor any French colonial architecture, and nor do I hear a word of French spoken. Also conspicuous by their absence are places of worship, which are still frowned upon by China's atheistic communist regime, although I do stumble across a small Buddhist temple in a side street.

Near Zhanjiang Central Station I stop for a glass of tea at a peasant woman's street stall. It's the best tea I've ever had, but, presumably because I'm a European visitor, she refuses to accept any money for it. This is a refreshing change from all the people who have tried to rip me off when I've worked abroad. Outside the station a cargo of caged ducks await the train quacking impatiently. Such a sight is no longer to be seen at stations in Britain, whose railways long ago stopped transporting livestock.

I ride the express train 160km (a hundred miles) inland to Yulin. Disappointingly my train is hauled by a Chinese State Railways diesel electric locomotive, the very last of China's magnificent sixteen wheeled steam locomotives having recently been withdrawn. With around five hundred working steam locomotives in preservation up and down the country, the British now have more working steam motive power than the Chinese. Chinese State Railways have left no trace of any water towers, coal yards or other steam locomotive paraphernalia. It's as if the organisation has wanted to obliterate the system's steam powered recent past as fast as possible. Tended by a train crew member, a charcoal brazier hisses away at the end of my carriage. Such an appliance would never pass muster with the Health and Safety Executive for use on a British train.

Line side gangs are hard at work every few kilometres, this single track railway line currently being converted in stages to double track. Such is the speed of China's industrialisation that the two tracks are certainly needed. I count four freight trains passing us heading south towards Zhanjiang in the space of an hour. The British invented the railways.

Even the system of flags, whistles and lanterns used as signals on the railways the world over were originally introduced onto the railways in the 1830s and 1840s by British Napoleonic War veterans who had used the same signalling media on the battlefield at Waterloo in 1815. But to our shame, in the second half of the twentieth century, much of our railway system closed and much of the rest allowed to decline into a shocking state of disrepair. Conversely the Chinese railway system and industry have expanded to the point where the Chinese rather than the British are today the world's premier exporters of railway technology.

A passenger train passes in the other direction, heading for the ferry that will transport it across the narrow stretch of sea separating mainland China from the island of Hainan. Passenger trains carried on ferries have been an extinct species in Britain since 1980. I remember as a child seeing one of the country's last, consisting of French carriages, at London's Victoria station.

Chinese towns are pockmarked by heavy industrial plants whose chimneys bilge acrid smoke into the atmosphere. We tend to forget that until the early nineteen eighties much of Britain and other counties that industrialised in the nineteenth century and deindustrialised in the late twentieth looked similar. Brits my age can still remember shipyards, steelworks and coalmines, some with steam shunting locomotives puffing away in their railway sidings. The legacy from that era can be witnessed in many hospitals, wherein lie, suffering from chronic respiratory diseases, thousands of elderly heavy industrial workers, the forgotten heroes of Britain's recent but now almost entirely obliterated industrial past.

The new so often sits uncomfortably and incongruously alongside the ancient in early twenty first century China. High rise buildings tower above traditionally clad peasants wading around in waterlogged paddy fields. The most bizarre sight to befall me from the train window is a Chinese peasant, in a straw hat, sitting on his ox cart, possessions by his side tied into bags on either end of a bamboo pole. The ox plods docilely along a muddy track bisecting a paddy field. The scene would look positively medieval were the peasant not shouting into a mobile phone.

Notable for its absence is the wildlife. In Britain, the traveller who takes the train east from Norwich in daylight will rarely fail to spot Chinese water deer hurtling away from the railway across the Broads, onto which they were introduced in the nineteenth century. The one place that anyone would expect to find Chinese water deer would be the lush wetlands of southern China. But here, as in many parts of the industrialising world, loss of habitat, population growth, farming and industrial pollution appear have taken their toll on wildlife.

In Yulin I stop at a cafe which is open to the street and order real Chinese food: shrimp and oriental vegetable soup. The food prepared and served by Britain's Chinese community doesn't approximate even remotely to what's served in China. I then visit a hairdresser's shop. I haven't seen another European all day, which probably explains why the hairdresser's assistant is filming me having my hair cut on her mobile phone, Europeans here being such a rarity. It also appears that in Yulin a man receives a free head, shoulder and hand massage with every haircut. I return to the ship more relaxed than at any other time during the voyage.

That night I sit watching, with its maps and symbols, the one thing on Chinese television that I can understand: the weather forecast.

Day 127

Muddy footprints have appeared on every toilet seat on the ship since we picked up Chinese crew members in Zhanjiang . It transpires that some Chinese crew members, having never used a Western style toilet before, have been standing on toilet seats and trying to balance, squat and pooh. Signs are now hastily printed and displayed in every toilet. These depict a diagonal red bar through a man attempting to balance and squat on a toilet seat. A crew member suggests that, as the nurse, it's my responsibility to teach the Chinese crew how to sit and pooh on a Western style toilet correctly.

The ship is somewhere off the coast of Indonesia. Having never sailed across the Equator before, I have to undergo an equatorial sailors' "initiation ceremony" on the deck of the ship as she traverses the Equator. I don't recall ever having to endure such a ceremony when crossing the Greenwich Meridian, even though as a child this was only a few hundred metres from my house.

I've tried hiding in a washroom, watching the water swirling down the washbasin's plughole, aware that we've crossed the Equator when the swirling changes direction. But it's no use, they've found me. The ceremony involves my crew mates tying me up and deluging me with foam, flour and a green slime whose ingredients nobody ever divulges to me and don't bear thinking about. I spend the rest of the day in the shower trying to liberate my body from this noxious concoction.

A steady procession of iron ore ships traverse the Indian Ocean between China and Australia. Those heading south are empty, those heading north heavily laden with Australian iron ore to feed China's burgeoning appetite for consumer goods. All have high pressure water cannons shooting from their gunwales. Presumably these are an attempt to thwart boarding and attack in this pirate infested ocean. But how much protection a bit of water would provide against a marauding bunch of hard nuts with heavy, hi tech weaponry I don't know.

Day 130

Surprisingly, considering our distance from land, off the Timorese coast we encounter what must be some of the largest dragonflies and flying beetles in existence. These are titanic dimensioned supersizers that one would have expected to have faced extinction long before the evolution of humankind. I've worked with many nurses in British hospitals who've asked me to catch little spiders and drop them outside. Maybe I should catch one of these flying monsters and take it home? "That little spider's nothing, love. Look at this!"

Day 133

We dock at Dampier, Western Australia. A pod of dolphins decides to entertain the three of us assembled on deck. They swim towards us then away on their backs, cackling as they do so.

The other two men are discussing domestic matters.

"If you want a divorce" remarks one to the other, "go to Haiti in the Caribbean. You can get a divorce without your wife's consent. While you're there you can get a Haitian witch doctor to put a voodoo curse on her an' all."

As I lie in my bunk that evening I drop off to sleep contemplating my long flight home the following day.

Peru

Day 1

Working as an expedition nurse is a role for which I've applied many times and been turned down. But I believe that for every success in life a person has to live through ten failures, and if a person isn't willing to try and fail ten times they'll never hit upon that one success. I've now finally been accepted.

I'm to be the nurse for a television film crew travelling deep into the heart of the Amazonian Rainforest in North East Peru. I've been working as an offshore nurse, but dolphins are normally considered to be sea mammals and they come up the Amazon, so I see no reason why I shouldn't join them.

Landing in Lima I'm driven along Avenue Fawcett, the highway from the airport to the city. I find riding along a road named after a British colonel who disappeared in the rainforest somewhat ominous and disconcerting. Fawcett was never seen again.

In common with the centres of many Latin American cities Lima has something of a Southern European ambience. Its wide streets and Spanish colonial architecture do little to acclimatise me for what lies ahead.

Whilst in Lima I'm warned that I must buy a net to erect over my sleeping bag. This should keep the rainforest's nocturnal, bloodsucking vampire bats away. On the theme of bloodsucking parasites I receive bad news from back in Britain. My Scottish bank, which shall remain nameless but whose initials stand for "Right Bunch of Shits" has closed down my account without any warning. I now have no means of retrieving my British savings.

Day 4

The terrain two days' travel from Lima and over a day's travel by canoe from the nearest airfield constitutes a completely different world. I arrive to discover that I must do my job with no electricity, no running water and no telecommunications.

The tribesmen in the rainforest village which is to be our home for the next two weeks welcome us with a bowl of an alcoholic brew. I'm told that this consists of fermented local fruit and human saliva. I take the tiniest sip that I think I can get away with then pass it on to the next person. I'm subsequently told by one of the film crew that the tribespeople noticed and are deeply offended by my unwillingness to ingest what they regard as an acceptable amount of fluid. Call me picky but I'd rather stick to a pint of British cask ale. And besides, I'm the film crew's nurse, so who's going to tend me if I fall ill when we're more than a day's travel from the nearest hospital?

Because oil companies have been exploiting and polluting neighbouring tracts of rainforest I'm told on no account to tell the tribespeople that I've worked as a nurse in the offshore oil and gas industry. As they only speak the local tribal language, and I only speak English and French, I can't envisage how that interaction is supposed to happen.

"Accommodation" for the entire film crew and myself consists of an open shelter with a thatched roof. The toilet is a hundred paces away in any direction. I hope that there aren't too many poisonous snakes around whenever I'm needing to bend down and go.

Before we entered the rainforest someone had the bright idea of packing the medical kit on an open backed pick up truck. When it pulled up at a road junction in a frontier logging town the locals thought it was Christmas. Having helped themselves to much of our medical kit we've arrived with only about half of what we need.

Day 5

The day begins at 4.45am when every cock in the village begins competing, crowing at the top of its voice, in response to the first chink of light in the sky.

A flock of red macaws glides gracefully and majestically across the river. Such a bird perched in a pet shop once told someone whom I detest intensely to piss off. I should have bought that creature.

I'm standing by the wood fire, eating a bowl of rice and yaca, a fruit grown widely across Latin America. I've gone vegetarian for the duration of this assignment. The tribeswoman who has been assigned to do our cooking has the unsavoury habit of strangling chickens in front of us, plucking them, throwing them in the cooking pot and serving them up two hours later. This has put me off meat altogether.

Just as a hedgehog, fox, badger or bird might visit a British back garden for a meal left out by a householder, semi domesticated rainforest monkeys and toucans hop around the village living off the tribespeople's scraps.

We have to trek into the rainforest to undertake some filming. Every cloud has a silver lining and I'm now beginning to realise that half the medical kit being stolen has one obvious advantage. One of the film crew tells me that he has worked with the veteran British wildlife television presenter Sir David Attenborough, who even at his great age was still taking his turn carrying the film equipment through the rainforest. And here I am, over forty years Sir David's junior, slip sliding around in rainforest mud with just one backpack. So I don't know how I would have managed carrying twice as much kit.

Later in the day, filming having been completed, I accidentally stumble upon the tribeswomen's bathing area in the river. Not wishing to incur the wrath of the tribal chief for having glimpsed his women folk in the near nude, and bearing in mind that the tribal chief has the authority to impose the sentence of death, I beat a hasty retreat. I've no plans to bathe in the river myself as I've no wish to meet a candiru, an Amazonian fish that can latch onto a person's urine stream and swim up their urethra. Never pee in the water when you're swimming in the Amazon.

One of the tribesmen points a gun at me as I walk through the village. I don't know why. Perhaps he saw me near the women's bathing area, perhaps he's the local medicine man fearing loss of business to me, or perhaps he's just having a laugh?

That night, as the clear, tropical sky and absence of any electric lighting reveal a cosmic display of thousands upon thousands of brilliantly sparking stars, the like of which I've never seen before.

Day 6

Once, whilst staying and working in Grimsby, a woman invited me back to her apartment in the town's East Marsh district, rated by many as the most deprived area in Britain. Whilst I was there her sixteen year old daughter and her daughter's boyfriend walked casually into the living room and lit up a crack pipe. With many of us who work struggling to find the money for a pint in the pub at the end of the week, from where these two teenagers acquired the money for this extortionately expensive pastime doesn't bear thinking about.

Politely making my excuses and leaving, I subsequently googled the woman's name and discovered that she'd been jailed for stabbing a man in the lungs with a screwdriver. Had I not departed when I had, on that occasion curiosity might well have killed the cat. The 2016 movie "Grimsby," which depicted the key character, Nobby Butcher, running up and down a bar with a firework rammed up his arse, was probably a sanitised and sterilised version of life in some parts of the town.

The apartment in Grimsby's East Marsh possessed running water, electricity, a washing machine and even a television set. The rude hut at the edge of the village into which I step this evening contains no such luxuries. But here in the rainforest much more extreme deprivation seems to be endured without a hint of dissent. There's no evidence of violence or illegal drug use here, although the crack cocaine that the Grimsby teenagers were smoking may well have been produced in this region.

I've been called to this hut to attend a boy who has been bitten by a spider. I try to find something about spider bites in the British National Formulary, the drugs directory used by all British nurses and doctors. But this is published in such small print that readers need the eyesight of a bird of prey to read it at the best of times. So in the pitch darkness of an Amazonian Rainforest night, hundreds of kilometres from the nearest mains electricity, I have no hope whatsoever of being able to make use of the book. A man in the hut translates from the local tribal language into Spanish and the film crew fixer interprets for me from Spanish into English. Most of the drugs having been stolen, I end up having to treat a bite from an unknown, venomous arachnid with paracetamol, an antihistamine and a topical cream. Those assembled seem happy enough with this, although my medical management would never have passed muster in a British hospital in a million years.

In the firelight I glance around the Spartan hut. Possessing no doors and windows it isn't even fully enclosed from the elements. Four small children huddle, harmoniously and without a hint of dissent, under one filthy rag that passes for a blanket. There's not a toy in sight, let alone an X Box or an I Pad.

I would give anything to exchange the harmony of this hovel for the permanent discord within my own apartment back in Britain. When I'm back at home I usually look after my daughter and her half sister's son. The two children, who despite being aunt and nephew are about the same age, would never dream of sharing a blanket or anything else. When they're together the verb "to share" doesn't even enter into their vocabulary. It seems that all they've ever done has been to punch each other's lights out. They've needed a boxing umpire to look after them instead of me.

You might expect a fight to break out between kids during a board game, but between these two the first fight invariably erupts even before the game starts, over who should have which coloured counter. When they started punching and kicking each other at London Zoo I threatened to throw them in the piranha fish tank, but even that didn't deter them. I've even known them to fight over a leaf.

Even when they were toddlers they'd bite each other, pull each other's hair and spit in each other's faces. As they've grown a little older the fights have become accompanied by ever more vicious verbal insults, delivered with an inordinate quantity of venom.

"YOU POOH POOH!"

WHACK!

"WAAAAAAH!"

A word used for "child" in Scotland and Northern England, "bairn," derives from the Norwegian word for child, "barn." A barn is exactly where these two kids belong.

I keep a calendar on my wall at home just to remind myself that it's not October 31st whenever I'm looking after them. We all know that Santa doesn't come to naughty children, but the last I heard he told Rudolf that he was imposing a three mile "no fly" zone around both of the kids' houses. I once had to complete a reference form for a friend applying for a job working with children. It asked:

"Would you entrust your children's care to this applicant?"

I answered:

"Give me a packing crate and I'll ship them to him right now."

He was offered the job but I never received my packing crate.

My daughter and her nephew must also have become the first pre school kids in British history to be barred from a pub; and in Blackpool too, which is a somewhat wild and saucy seaside resort where people's behaviour is pretty decadent at the best of times. So that really did take some doing. They hurtled into the toilet, slamming and locking the door in my face before I could pursue them. A minute or two after they re emerged, the pub landlord presented me with about ten metres (thirty feet) of toilet tissue that they'd unravelled and thrown on the floor.

"LOOK WHAT THEY'VE DONE!"

He then pointed to the exit.

This has been far from the only time that I've wished that the ground would open up and swallow me when I've been accompanying the kids.

On another occasion we were waiting on a platform for a train when the children decided to ask the somewhat portly station master if he was the Fat Controller. I also once took them to Southern England's Arundel Castle, whose near namesake features in their favourite children's film, "Frozen." The castle was full of little girls dressed as Princess Elsa and Princess Anna looking bitterly disappointed that the real Elsa and Anna weren't in residence. My daughter and her nephew behaved like Satan's children that day; Beelzebub's very own offspring. As I was leading them away in complete disgrace, a woman stopped me.

"Excuse me, I think those children are lovely, and I think the way you're speaking to them really is quite rude."

"I don't care what you think. Go and jump off that parapet."

Have you ever seen the look of shock and surprise on a piece of road kill's face? Never push a parent's buttons when they're at the end of their tether. There's always some lippy, politically correct cow who thinks that she knows better than the parent, isn't there?

Because I believe that anyone wishing to try and truly understand their own place in the world needs to see something of it, I tell the children that, when they're about sixteen and before they start making university and career choices, I'd like to take them on a long trip to visit as many countries as possible. But the success of any such trip would hinge upon them not killing each other before we've left Europe or even our departure airport.

Alice in Wonderland (1852-1934) and Christopher Robin in the "Winnie the Pooh" stories (1920-1996) were real British children. My daughter and her nephew too are now being immortalised in a book, but for all the wrong reasons. If you ever see me ruffle the kids' hair it's not out of affection but to make sure that they haven't started growing horns out of the tops of their heads.

I'm sure that these four little children huddled under the blanket in the rainforest hut before me could teach my daughter and her nephew a thing or two about familial love and harmony. And I don't suppose that they've been barred from any pubs either. Maybe my daughter and her nephew should be transported from Britain to live in the rainforest with these harmonious siblings for a couple of months? Although how my daughter and her nephew would cope with no television, computer or other comforts of twenty first century life I don't know.

Day 20

We're homeward bound, and I'm leaving the rainforest without, disappointingly, having seen a jaguar, tapir or any other native large mammal during my stay. The cameraman assures me that a spectator can wait for a week to spot a particular wild large mammal and still have no luck, not just in the Amazonian Rainforest but in most parts of the world, such has been the free fall in biodiversity across the globe in recent decades.

After a day's journey down river we arrive at a small hotel whose running water offers me the first chance in over two weeks to rid myself of rainforest mud. Feeling clean again after so long fills me with a sense of elation. "You're an ABBA fan are you?" the producer remarks to me that evening. "I could hear you singing 'Dancing Queen' in the shower."

The local barber trims my hair entirely by hand. The town's diesel generator is switched off so there's no electricity. He charges me less than a pound, a euro or even an American dollar for one of the most thorough haircuts I've ever received.

Day 21

It's the day before we return to Europe and we're at a hotel a short distance from Lima Airport. I take the public bus, a decrepit Chevrolet ex American school bus, into the city. I struggle as I ask for my fare. I don't profess to speaking fluent or even conversational Spanish and, whereas English is widely spoken in Africa and Asia, in Latin America Spanish and Portuguese are the lingua francas. The on board sound system blasts out a repertoire of nineteen eighties and nineteen nineties British and American pop songs. On the front seat lies an unattended baby who I can only assume is either the driver's or the conductor's. Conductors appear to have several functions on Peruvian buses. As well as collecting the fares they stand at the doors of the bus and call out its destination, many Peruvians being illiterate and therefore unable to read signage. It also appears to be the conductor's function to beat up opponents from any vehicle with which the bus collides. When we pass another bus rather too closely, clipping its side and removing its wing mirror, the respective buses' conductors disembark and proceed to remonstrate in the middle of the road. A fight breaks out. My daughter and her nephew could learn a technique or two from these two combatants.

Day 23

More than twenty four hours sitting on the hard seat of the motorised canoe travelling back out of the rainforest has left me with a pressure sore on my backside. I'd quite happily stand on the KLM Royal Dutch Airlines flight from Lima back to Amsterdam if they'd let me.

Arriving in Amsterdam, having several hours before my connecting flight, I pay the city centre a visit. After buying an ice cream I inadvertently wander into the city's infamous red light district. Observing me licking my ice cream from her booth a prostitute emerges and invites me to lick something else.

Landing back in Britain later that day I proceed through the airport's customs. As I fumble amongst the Peruvian shrapnel in my money belt to try to retrieve some British shrapnel for my bus fare a customs officer halts me.

"Could I ask where you've just come from Sir?"

"South America via Amsterdam," I reply, without pausing to remember that these are two of the world's most notorious places for illicit narcotics production and misuse.

The customs officer produces a pair of rubber gloves. Welcome home! It's "bend over boy" time.

www.ingramcontent.com/pod-product-compliance
Lightning Source LLC
Chambersburg PA
CBHW070954080526
44587CB00015B/2311